TEACH ME
WHAT
MAMA
DIDN'T
KNOW

TEACH ME WHAT MAMA DIDN'T KNOW

ANGELA BAKER-WARD

TEACH ME WHAT MAMA DIDN'T KNOW

Copyright © 2018 Angela Baker-Ward.

All rights reserved. No part of this book may be used or reproduced by any means, graphic, electronic, or mechanical, including photocopying, recording, taping or by any information storage retrieval system without the written permission of the author except in the case of brief quotations embodied in critical articles and reviews.

Unless otherwise indicated, all scripture quotations are from The Holy Bible, English Standard Version® (ESV®). Copyright ©2001 by Crossway Bibles, a division of Good News Publishers. Used by permission. All rights reserved.

Scripture quotations marked MSG are taken from THE MESSAGE. Copyright © 1993, 1994, 1995, 1996, 2000, 2001, 2002, 2003 by Eugene H. Peterson. Used by permission of NavPress Publishing Group. Website.

iUniverse books may be ordered through booksellers or by contacting:

iUniverse
1663 Liberty Drive
Bloomington, IN 47403
www.iuniverse.com
1-800-Authors (1-800-288-4677)

Because of the dynamic nature of the Internet, any web addresses or links contained in this book may have changed since publication and may no longer be valid. The views expressed in this work are solely those of the author and do not necessarily reflect the views of the publisher, and the publisher hereby disclaims any responsibility for them.

Any people depicted in stock imagery provided by Getty Images are models, and such images are being used for illustrative purposes only. Certain stock imagery © Getty Images.

ISBN: 978-1-5320-5510-2 (sc)
ISBN: 978-1-5320-5509-6 (e)

Library of Congress Control Number: 2018910232

Print information available on the last page.

iUniverse rev. date: 08/31/2018

Dedications

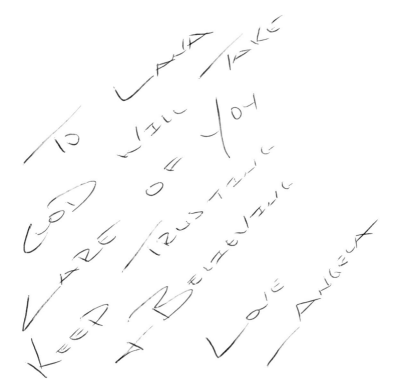

To Lana Jake
God Will You
Care of
Keep Trusting
& Believing
Love Angela

First and foremost, to you the reader. It is my sincere prayer that you let no one keep you from experiencing real love, real joy, and real peace. No abuser, no accuser, and no user should have the power to keep you silent or suppressed. You have what it takes to live to the fullest your predestined, abundant life. You also have what it takes to live an amazing life. Speak into the atmosphere!

To women in my lineage: my lovely mother, Barbara; my grandmothers Frances and Queenie; and my beloved great-grandmother Hattie. All in their own way are considered women of honor, strength, and courage.

To those who support Ward Ministries, under which this book is written, and to my Morning Expresso team, Barthenia, Donna, and Kiesha, thank you for years of praying together, studying God's Word together, and constant, unfailing love and support.

To my second mom and aunt, the fabulous Beverly J. I have not the words to express to you the love I have for you. God put you in a position to guide me toward a better life. You didn't have to do it, but you chose to, and you did. You helped save my life, and for that I am forever grateful.

To my mother-in-love, Ursula, when it's my time, I pray I'm close to half the amazing mom-mom you are. Thank you for being a woman of wisdom, laughter, love, and kindness.

To my daughter, Kimberly. Though I pray I have not failed you as a mother, I desire wholeheartedly for you to become an even greater mom than I am. God made you beautiful inside and out for a reason. Go conquer the world!

To my husband, my lover, my ultimate best friend, Daniel. Thanks for believing in me, thanks for encouraging me, and thanks for picking me up from where the rest of the world dropped me off. You are definitely the best that ever did it!

To my handsome sons, my Brian and my Kenneth. Run on sons and see what the end is going to be. I am grateful to God for the blessings He has bestowed over your lives. Continue to boldly believe in and pursue your dreams and goals. You got this!

To my father-in-love, William J., my instant dad, you have no idea how much your example of prayer, provision, and protection for your family has brightened my life.

In loving memory of my dad, Sherman V. Rest in peace. You are sorely missed.

To my sister Stephanie and all my sister-friends, Avery, Chavon, Donna, Glenda, Ingrid, Karlessa, Lakesha, LaTina, Nona, Sonya, Tara L., Tereda, Trina, and Tyquese. Thank you for being true friends and teaching me how to be a friend in return.

To my brothers, Alexandro, Lewis, and Gregory, to God be the glory for all the wonderful things He has done in your lives. I am proud of the men you have become and proud you have been my lifelong friends.

I cannot end this dedication without mentioning my godchildren and those whose parents allow them to call me Mama Ang. Here's to you too, Admed, Brian, Landon, Langston, Logan, Myron, Ni' Eymah, Rodney, Samala, Shai-Anne, and Shawn. Continue to aim high. Stay strong and stand bold on the Word of God.

To all my nieces and nephews and my future grands, promise me you will never let the world make you feel less than great. I pray you will always see yourself and your future through the eyes of God. I believe in you. Stand strong, be bold, stay courageous, be great, and live out loud!

Contents

Preface xiii
Introduction xvii

Self-Love 1
   Love Yourself 3
   Life Gets Better 7
   Live Life Abundantly 18

Friends, Family, and Them 23
   Who Are They? 25
   Who Are You? 28
   They Can Hurt You 31
   Consequences 36
   Dream Killers 39

Fleeing Temptation 45
   Keep the Lord's Covenant 47
   Declare Purity 51
   Be Steadfast 54
   80 – 18 = 62 59

Marriage and Parenting 65
   How Long Should You Wait? 67
   Seek God's Counsel 72
   Pray without Ceasing 78

Money 81
    Be a Great Steward 83
    Personal Finance 87
    Minimalism 90
    It's Okay to Say No 96
    Maintain Good Credit............................ 99

Religion versus Relationship 109
    Traditions... 111
    God Loves You 119

Rewrite the Script..123
    Getting Directions..................................125
    Never Too Late.......................................133

Notes 139

Preface

This book is for those who have been weighed down by life. It's perfect for both individual and group studies. It helps mentors show mentees that starting over is possible. It shows everyone that, yes, you can leave a life of abuse and hopelessness and live a life full of love, joy, and peace.

It's also for those who have been abandoned, abused, neglected, and rejected. This book brings hope to those who have struggled and to those who feel they are traveling alone in the world of adulthood.

It is my desire that everyone reading this book will prosper in health—physically, spiritually, emotionally, and mentally—and in wealth.

Through these pages, you will discover that I am a survivor of abuse, neglect, and many other things.

Car Accident

One day while driving to work, traffic on the highway came to a sudden stop. My car was hit hard from the rear and pushed into the car in front of me. Because of the impact to my car, I experienced extreme nausea, a pounding head, and a constant spinning sensation. As the CEO of MyTechnicalFriend.com, I was instructed to stay off computers and technical gadgets and to refrain from watching TV or talking on the phone for longer than fifteen minutes at a time. I had a whole list of *thou shall nots* from my attending doctors. My back, my neck, my chest, my stomach, my whole body was out of whack because of the accident, and some of the doctors told me that the only thing that would help was rest.

As I was lying in bed resting, I could hear the Lord, clear as day, say, "Do you have time now to do what I've been asking you to do?" So here it is—this book, my assignment from God. No, I hadn't been running from the assignment, but I had been telling the Lord I had no time. I'm a wife, a mother, a full-time employee, and a full-time student, and I have my own business. I'm a First Lady, a minister, a choir director, a Sunday school teacher, a counselor and adviser to many; the list goes on and on. So, as far as I could see, there was no free time, and my constant response to the Lord was "I'll get to it when I have the time."

Because of the accident, for a little over two months, I was written out of work from my doctors, and the Lord kept saying during those months, "The time is now."

Giving Birth to This Book

One day, my husband, Daniel, woke up and said, "Babe, I had a dream you were pushing out a baby."

My response was "The only baby I'm pushing out is this book." *So, Lord, let's do this!*

For years, I knew the title, *Teach Me What Mama Didn't Know*, well before I knew all the content. The word *Mama* in the title does not refer just to my biological mother; it refers to all the adults, both male and female, who I wish could've better prepared me for life as an adult. Nevertheless, as I started penning the pages that follow, I discovered a dilemma. The dilemma was what I knew I needed to write about versus what some people needed me to write about. I wanted to write about things I wish I had been taught so I could have been better prepared for life as an adult. Others needed me to write about overcoming the scars of my past, the results of sexual, physical, mental, verbal, and emotional abuse. It's a past that, every now and then, still creeps into my present world. I've gotten over the physical, the mental, the emotional, and the verbal abuse, but if truth be told, I seem to only be perhaps 75 percent over the sexual abuse. I don't know why I still cringe when I see people hold children a certain way and when I see children sitting on the laps of men. I don't know why I carefully choose the words I say to ensure they won't be taken in a sexual context. I don't know why I am not able to put an adjective to how I feel about the sexual situations some adults put me in as a child. I'm not angry, not sad, not depressed, but there is definitely a void I cannot describe.

Though pain from sexual, physical, mental, verbal, and emotional abuse was once my story, my sincere desire is that you too can say, as my good friend and gospel recording artist Karlessa Beach sings in her song, "In a New Place,"

I dealt with the pain—
Now joy has came.
I'm in a new place,
So grateful for the change,
So grateful for Your grace.
I'm in a new place,
A brand-new place!

Introduction

Parents, guardians, mentors, friends, and loved ones, sometimes when you care for others and desire to avoid confrontation, discussing topics like abuse, self-love, temptation, money management, parenting, and religion can be challenging—as is talking about funeral arrangements. Let this book be used in those times when verbal conversations are difficult. Here are some great ways to open the dialogue for those kinds of situations:

1) Share the chapters in this book that closely pertain to the situation at hand with the children and people in your life you care about. Ask them to read those chapters. This will make for a smooth transition into dialoguing.
2) Pray and openly discuss the situation and chapters together.

As stated in the preface, I have not been able to settle on an adjective to describe how I feel about the scars of my past. I often find it best to not even think on it. The coping process I have adopted is, *Why sit in the frying pan of agony when I have the freedom to stay out of it?* However, when the sexual abuse does cross my mind, I recall that it started well before my kindergarten year. It ended sometime after seventh grade. No matter where I went, state to state, place to place, there was always someone wanting to show me pleasures my body could experience. When I think on these things, I feel guilt and shame. How did I not fully comprehend that what my body was experiencing at such a young age was wrong? At what point did my mind become a willing participant, acting as if the situation was right? How did I let it go on for so long? Why do I remember praying to God, asking Him to make me ugly, hoping I would become invisible? Why did the encounters turn into violence? Why did the adults who should have known better never apologize? When I tried to bring it to the light, why was I called a liar? Why didn't everyone take the time to heal? Are others also living with guilt and shame? Why did I recently learn about someone who is near to my heart experiencing a much greater violation? Why do I wonder if knowing this is supposed to make what I went through all right? Will this void ever go away? Why would I much rather not think about it?

Why do I still want to know? Will God ever grant us the opportunity to come together and heal? Again, why would I much rather not think about it?

In addressing the dilemma, this book intertwines healing from my past with helping others prepare for a brighter future. I pray that no matter where you are in life, you forgive not only others but yourself as well. Rewrite the script and claim your freedom!

I have learned that when I cover all my situations as God does (extending grace and mercy), I live with true love, joy, and perfect peace. When I try to remove the blanket of grace and mercy I've extended to others, hate, sadness, and a mind full of unrest try to take over.

I may have some scars, but I purposely choose to march forth and operate with the fruit of the Spirit (Galatians 5:22–23). It doesn't downplay the fact that a great disservice was done in my past; it allows me to not walk around with the chains from Satan that tried to keep me bound.

I fully understand that others can go through the same kind of situation but heal differently. I believe it's okay to visit the grave of your wound; just don't stay there too long. Whatever you have endured in your life, true healing starts when you *purposely* choose to operate from a place of peace. If you are a victim of abuse and trauma and are looking to reclaim your love, joy, and peace, know this: there was a certain man in the Bible who had an infirmity for thirty-eight years. I ask you, like Jesus asked him in John 5:6 (ESV), "Do you want to be healed?" Then in John 5:8 (ESV): "Jesus said to him, Get up, take up your bed, and walk."

Because of all the sexual, physical, mental, verbal, and emotional abuse I endured growing up, many people in my family have come to me through the years and have said in various ways and verbatim, "I'm surprised you didn't go crazy." Let me tell you—I can remember during a time in my life praying to God, asking Him to allow me to go crazy so I wouldn't be aware of the things that were happening to me. I can still recall His response: "If they are treating you this way while you are sane, imagine how they will treat you if you are insane." I changed my mind-set in that moment and asked the Lord to help me rise above my situation.

Please—I beg of you—rise above the situations you have encountered or will encounter. Walk toward your prosperous destiny. Don't let the enemy steal another moment of your joy. Claim your victory. Declare it and speak it:

> I will remain the head and not the tail!
> I will remain above and not beneath!
> I will always purposely rise above
> challenging situations!
> I will not let the enemy steal another second of my joy!
> This is the day the Lord has made for me. I will
> rejoice and be glad in every second of it!
> I am more than a conqueror. I am a victorious winner!

Speak into the Atmosphere Prayer

"Father God, thank You for teaching me about Your perfect peace. I will walk this Christian journey by faith and not by sight. I will always look to You, the true source of all my help. I will speak life over every situation I encounter. I will always deal with others from a place of love, peace, and joy. In Jesus's name. Amen."

Special Note

Above all titles given to me as a Christian—First Lady, counselor, choir director, and youth director, among many others—I narrow them all down to I am a follower of Jesus the Christ. Therefore, most of my advice comes from what I have been taught from the heavenly Father through meditating on His Word and prayer. You will discover that my advice for nearly everything that follows consists in part of informing you to pray. My situations and my life will not match your situation and life exactly. Though the solutions to our concerns may be similar, they will not be exact. Why not? Because God has a specific plan designed especially for you. He knows *exactly* what you need. So again, my advice above everything is for you to pray to the Lord about all things. The Bible tells us that the prayer of a righteous person has great power. If you are unsure how to pray, there is an online resource by Christian Word Ministries at www.christianword.org. They also have an app called "Prayer Book" by Christian Word Ministries.

If you are just starting in your prayer journey, ACTS is an acronym to help cover the basics to prayer:

> A = Adoration: "Lord God, I honor, reverence, and acknowledge You as Lord over all, as well as Lord over my life."
>
> C = Confessions: "I ask You, Father, to forgive me of my sins—the things I've said, done, and

thought that are not pleasing in Your sight. Help me to do what is right, and as You forgive me, help me to also forgive others."

T = Thanksgiving: "God, thank You for all the blessings you have given me. Thank You for extending to me salvation, love, peace, joy, faith, and hope."

S = Supplication: "Thank You for meeting my daily needs. In Jesus's name. Amen."

Self-Love

Matthew 22:37-40 (ESV)

Love Yourself

And he said to him, "You shall love the Lord your God with all your heart and with all your soul and with all your mind. This is the great and first commandment. And a second is like it: You shall love your neighbor as yourself. On these two commandments depend all the Law and the Prophets."
—Matthew 22:37–40 (ESV)

I was in the sixth grade when I realized what being a girlie girl meant. All the other middle school girls in my class had apparently already figured this out. They would come to school with makeup on, all their hairs seemingly in place, and with what appeared to be just the right words to get the cutest boys. I was somewhat of a tomboy, so I'd show up to school like *whatever*, eagerly awaiting lunchtime so I could participate in the card game of spades. Playing cards and reading books were my mental escapes from reality.

It was also while in the sixth grade I discovered "Oh my, we're supposed to have boobies?" As I sit here and type, I begin to shed tears, not because my sixth-grade body lacked boobies (though it did, and cotton balls and tissue were my best stuffed-bra accessories back in the day). I shed tears because when I started seriously penning this book, my daughter was in the sixth grade—and dear Lord, where has time gone? It is my ultimate goal to ensure she knows the things her mama didn't know, like how important it is to love herself.

Love is a powerful word with many forms. As you grow into adulthood, you come to experience four different types of love: *agape*, *phileo*, *storge*, and *eros*. Agape is unconditional love; this is the love a parent may have for a child, or siblings may have for one another. Agape looks past a person's flaws. Phileo chooses to have more affection toward someone. This is the kind of love you may have toward a best friend. Storge is the love that helps you forgive a person time and time again; it's the love that says, "I don't have to like what you do, but I do have to love you." Storge is the kind of love you might have for those who do you wrong. Eros is a romantic love, the kind a husband has toward his wife and vice versa. If you're in elementary school, middle school, or high school, trust me—you can wait until later in your life for eros.

Self-Love

By the time I was in sixth grade, none of those loves meant anything to me. However, the love I wish I had known about is self-love. Several verses in the Bible teach us to love our neighbor as ourselves. One is found in Matthew 22:39 (ESV): "love your neighbor as yourself."

Trust me when I say I didn't have a problem loving others; it was me who was missing out on love, the love from me. There was no self-love. Don't get me wrong; I thought I was cute—at times, that is. I was very smart, and I had friends (so I thought), but I let people do things and say things, treating me any kind of way. What did I do in return? I gave them agape love. Truthfully, I gave everyone storge love. I was always willing to quickly forgive, forget, and dust off the pieces—a "let's just act like it never happened" type of love. I loved everyone unconditionally, flaws and all. Spit on me; I still loved you. Talk about me badly; I still loved you. Lie on me; I still loved you. I was abused sexually, physically, mentally, verbally, and emotionally, but I still loved. The consequences I endured from not having self-love went well into my grown-up years. I barely survived because I did not know I was supposed to love myself. The glue that held me together all those years was, around the age of twelve, when I was in sixth grade, I was introduced to a man named Jesus, my King of kings, my Lord of lords, my Savior, my Father, my true friend. Though I was getting to know Jesus and even now am getting to know

> **IT WAS ME WHO WAS MISSING OUT ON LOVE**
>
> #TMWMDK

Teach Me What Mama Didn't Know

Him more and more, I was still lacking self-love, which in my opinion is totally different from self-esteem. See, I thought I was cute and smart. I had plenty self-esteem, but I let others treat me however they wanted to, and therefore I lacked self-love.

Life Gets Better

I never got to experience what it was like to be a girlie girl. I didn't regret it then, but I do now. Back then, I was too busy saving those who were supposed to keep me safe. I was always loving and doing things for those who couldn't care less if I lived or died. Don't get me wrong, I don't regret the love I gave people. I regret not being taught what it meant to love myself. It seems as though we have become a society that chooses to forget about the delicacy of a girl. We want them to toughen up, have them stop crying and quickly get over situations that are causing them to hurt. Well, that mind-set is the beginning of robbing the little child of the idea of self-love. Today, I look around and see so much evidence of young ladies who were never taught the importance of self-love. The things I see them do, all for the love and affection of others breaks my heart. Letting others treat them as doormats, dressing provocatively, and being rowdy with the intent to be noticed seems to be the norm. As parents, guardians, mentors, and adults, we've got to remember to choose our actions and words wisely when dealing with those who are following in our footsteps.

Teach Me What Mama Didn't Know

While I was growing up, various adults, with hatred and in demeaning ways, said things like "Get your ass over there somewhere and sit down," "Stop all that damn noise; nobody wants to hear that," and "Do it your damn self!" Over time, words like that toughen you up. You start looking to do everything yourself, you stop shedding tears, and you shut down, no longer able to express what you're feeling with those who come around and really love you. My husband describes me as having an independent spirit. He reminds me often to come out of survivor mode. When I'm in survivor mode, it can appear to others as if I've gone into a trance, where it's just me in this world and no one else. No, you cannot help me, you cannot fix this, and I must do this myself. It's almost how a person with obsessive-compulsive disorder does not want you to touch their things. When I'm in survivor mode, I do not want anyone to touch the things pertaining to my life. Unfortunately, the little girl inside of me always pushes everyone away and reverts to survivor mode when the going gets tough. Shutting down and resorting to survivor mode can be one of the lingering consequences people endure when they don't know the importance of self-love. Self-love reminds me that things about me and my life do not have to be perfect. Self-love reminds me to chill, relax, and reflect on the positives.

My prayer is that you understand the extreme importance of self-love. Maybe you have already been thrown into a cycle of self-hate. As it is the opposite of

Self-Love

self-love, you can reverse the negatives and experience true self-love. I got to a point in my life where I said, "Enough is enough. Enough of letting others talk to me in a demeaning way, treating me as if I'm someone of no importance." I am a Christian, and through studying God's Word, I realized that in His eyes, I have equal rights, no matter what anyone else thinks. Through proactively gaining a closer relationship with the Lord, I realized I *am* who He says I am. I am the head and not the tail, above and not beneath.

Now, it took me some time to realize that the only opinion of me that matters is the Lord's; I was married with kids when the light bulb came on. The bottom line is I took myself out of the cycle of self-hate, and you can too. How? First, join with others and study God's Word; get to know Jesus as your Lord and Savior. Second, stand boldly on Philippians 4:6, "Do not be anxious about anything." Third, understand the Serenity Prayer:

> God grant me the serenity to accept
> the things I cannot change,
> Courage to change the things I can,
> And wisdom to know the difference.

Below is a list of ten things I did not like about myself at one point in my life. These weren't ideas of self-hate I just woke up with one day. These are things that were said to me in my childhood, and I took notice and agreed with someone that they were unsatisfactory.

Teach Me What Mama Didn't Know

1) My boobs	2) My looks
3) My hair	4) My shoe size
5) My forehead	6) My weight
7) My teeth	8) My voice
9) My life's worth	10) My mental state

As a kid, these things can appear to be the differences between life and death. Even for adults, some of these things are monumental. Sometimes as an adult, if you haven't been freed from the scars of the past, those things can spring feelings of insecurity.

Here's where the Serenity Prayer comes into play.

Item 1: my itty bitties (boobs, that is). I spent my whole childhood doing the "I must, I must, I must increase my bust" exercise. Some of you are probably doing it right now. Some are probably searching the internet to see exactly what it is. Let me inform you: it doesn't work. Trust me. If it did, I wouldn't be boobless. I could not increase the size of my boobs; it was one of the things I could not change, so I had to accept it and move on. Truth be told, most adult women with big boobs wish they could decrease the size of their boobs because of the pain and discomfort it causes them. But let's roll back a little. Why was it so important for me to have bigger breasts? Because it was an idea placed in my head. It definitely wasn't something I thought of on my own. Someone calling me flat chested or some other girl getting all the attention because she looked as though she had soccer balls for breasts made me look at mine and label them as unacceptable. I used to think if I had

Self-Love

the money, I would have surgery to get bigger breasts. If that's your thought as well, remember we are aiming for self-love. If someone doesn't like you or accept you because you are not the size they desire you to be, either they need a new focus in their view of you or they need to move on. Trust me—they are not worth your time. God made you who you are. There are plenty of people who will accept the you God made you to be. Don't get caught up in anyone's idea of what you should look like.

Item 2: my looks. How many times and ways can a girl be told she's ugly? Even if it's done in a joking manner, it hurts, especially if mom and dad aren't there to pick up the pieces. Or even worse, if the mom and dad are the ones pronouncing to their child that he or she is ugly, well, it just gets uglier from there (no pun intended). I'm laughing now, but I can't tell you how many, "You so ugly" jokes I heard growing up. "You so ugly, when you step in the mirror, it begs for the electric chair." I mean really—that's got to be some kind of ugly when the mirror wants to die. Like I said, I'm laughing now, but those sayings were not funny when I was a child. So what did I do? I spent time trying to figure out how to wear globs of makeup.

Was it something I could change? I thought I could. I thought I *needed* to—with makeup. However, as I got older and learned to accept me as I am, I realized I'm a beautiful woman, and I'm not just saying it either. You be the judge. Flip over to the back cover and check me out. Again, it was planted in my head that I was ugly; I didn't just wake up with the idea of ugliness.

Teach Me What Mama Didn't Know

People can be cruel, and it usually has nothing to do with you. Most of the time, it's their own shortcomings and embedded judgments. To reverse how you feel about yourself (which in turn reverses how others feel about you), quickly accept you for you. Yes, I know it sounds easier said than done, but I am a living witness. I know it works.

Start accepting everything about yourself. If you're short, tall, fat, or skinny, if you have acne, small teeth, large hands—whatever it is, accept it. Stop flinching and showing others that their words of nonacceptance affect you. Start boldly saying, "I like that about me," and watch them quickly start letting you be who God intended you to be.

START BOLDLY SAYING, "I LIKE THAT ABOUT ME"

#TMWMDK

On the flip side, you can also be the person pointing out negative attributes about yourself that others just don't see. For example, at one point, I would say to my husband or closest friends things like "I'm getting fat. I'm aging rapidly," and they would look at me as if some alien had taken over my mouth. My husband would actually get offended, as if I was some outsider throwing insults on his wife. The bottom line is there are people who truly love you. Most importantly, God loves you. I encourage you to seek His face through prayer and studying the Bible to ensure you are who He intended you to be.

Let's be honest. There are some not-as-gorgeous people in the world. But I've seen some of them get some of the most beautiful spouses. How? One, because

Self-Love

they don't see themselves as ugly. Two, true love doesn't connect with a face; it connects with the heart. Three, they have great self-love for themselves. Love yourself!

Item 3: my hair. It still puzzles me today how my mother has some of the silkiest prettiest, long strands of hair. I inherited Barb and Wire. My hair is so thick I could get a perm and permanent hair color on the same day, and it wouldn't fall out. (Note: a perm and permanent hair color should never be done on the same day or even within a few weeks of each other, as you may go bald.) Now, ask me what's worse—being called nappy head or having your bangs always sticking straight up in the air? Honestly, I don't have an answer. They both can be pretty stressful for a child.

Flashback, pause, rewind. I just had a memory of my mother putting about ten ponytails with ribbons in my hair. I was fourteen at the time, heading to high school. That many ponytails and ribbons are for elementary school kids. Dear Lord, I have no idea what she was thinking. I think I was in the tenth or eleventh grade when I eventually got a perm. I was tired of being the girl with the poufy hair. Ever since, I've done whatever I feel like doing with my hair. It's been long, super short, natural, relaxed, and extended—whatever I felt like doing.

I've been on a natural hair journey for a several years now. It's not because I have the mentality of "I'm nappy by nature." It's because it's *my* barbwire. I do what I want, take it or leave it. I have a choice. I can choose to let my hair be long and straight down my back, I can rock my natural curls, or I can pick my afro out. People still ask me daily, "What are you doing to your hair now?" My response is "What I choose to do." Let your choices be yours, not because you were pressured to fit in. Choose to be the person God made you to be. Love you as God loves you.

Items 4 and 5: my shoe size and my forehead. We're not even going to go there. God gave them to me, and I accept that, yes, I have a larger forehead than the average barely-has-a-forehead person. I don't notice it when I look in the mirror though. Why? Because I choose not to dwell on it. When you choose not to dwell on something, it makes other people no longer take notice. As for my feet, I have very pretty feet. I used to wish they were smaller because I was fed the idea that smaller feet are better. But really, they are just feet. I use them to walk on; that is all.

Items 6 and 7: my weight and my teeth. Before I had children, I was always a very skinny person. Oddly, I never saw myself as skinny, not until I looked back at pictures of me in my younger days. People calling me skinny never bothered me because, again, I never saw myself as skinny. What you choose to focus on will alter your focus. If you focus on being pretty, you will be pretty. If you focus on being ugly, you guessed it. Don't focus on negativity.

Notice how I said that *before I had children*, I was skinny; well, that's no longer the case. No, I'm not currently breaking the scale, but according to the doctor's height and weight chart, I'm considered obese. So I ask

Self-Love

myself, Do I let the word *obese* bring me down? Do I see myself as obese? Is this something I can and am willing to change? Do I love myself enough to change it for me? I don't see myself as obese. I see myself as just right. However, I know that to stay healthy and live a good, long life for those I love and who in return love me, I've got to do something to turn the obesity label around. I choose to eat right and exercise—not because society loves looking at super-skinny women but because I want to live a healthy, long life. Again, it's my choice.

Now, I've been called Bugs Bunny and bucktooth because I have rather large teeth. Again, God gave them to me. They are mine, so I accept them. If you choose to change your teeth, that's up to you, but don't let it be because you're trying to fit in. As an adult, I decided to wear braces—not because I was trying to meet society's beauty standard of straight teeth but because years ago I'd had my wisdom teeth pulled out and then my teeth shifted. I made the decision to shift them back before they became a horrible mess by the time I had grandchildren and scared them to death. It's a choice I made out of self-love.

As for item 8, my voice, I've sang for as far back as I can remember. And as far back as I can remember, there were peers who would try to discredit my ability to sing pleasantly. At the time, I didn't know they were just playfully joking. If I had let their words, such as "you sound like a dying cat," stop me, I would never have experienced the many offers I had to go into the studio and sing on radio stations. And no, I don't sound like a dying cat. People can be little bullies even while joking. You must believe in your own abilities. Improve upon your skills if you must, but don't let people keep you from doing what you love.

Item 9, my life's worth. As a child, I had an adult tell me, "Die already!" Trust me. I tried several times, and God spared me. If you are considering ending it all, pay attention and listen carefully: *life ... gets ... better. Your life is worth the living. You must learn self-love.* It may seem hard at first, like learning to ride a bike, but daily I challenge you to get to know God the Father. Remind yourself that you are according to God, the head and not the tail, above and not beneath. You are more than a conqueror; you can do all things through Christ who strengthens you.

Item 10, my mental state. I was recently informed that when I was a child, some people found pleasure in laughing while labeling me as retarded. Now, it's one thing when kids are joking around, calling each other retarded. It's a totally different thing when adults call you retarded and treat you as such. When I found that out, it was like the world was about to end. I was good and grown, in my late thirties. That news brought back horrible childhood memories, which led me to focus on the way I used to be treated. That, in turn, led me to believe I was being treated so horribly because they thought I couldn't tell the difference. Imagine what being called retarded does to a person's mind-set. However, I've healed from that and boldly now say, "He who laughs last laughs best." Yes, I'm sitting here in full laughter. Imagine

Self-Love

that—me, an army veteran, with college degrees and an amazing career, married with kids and a whole host of friends and family who all see the beauty in me.

Now, for you, let's change the negatives to positives. Write down five things that have *you* bothered about yourself. Immediately next to the negative, change it to a positive.

Turn Your Negative	To a Positive
Example: My ears	I can hear, and they fit my face.
1)	1)
2)	2)
3)	3)
4)	4)
5)	5)

From this day forth, aim to reflect on the positives.

Live Life Abundantly

One day while driving home with my daughter, she said to me with a serious look on her face and a voice cracking with concern, "Mom, can you keep driving? I have some things I need to ask you." That led to four hours of driving on random roads so she could get out everything she needed to discuss. She asked me for advice about all the possible pressures in her everyday life. While she was speaking, I was praying that God would give me the right words to say, and in my desire to keep it transparent, open, and honest, I gave her advice from a heart full of God's Word and my newfound self-love.

Months later, I asked her what she got from our conversation, and this is what she said: "The most important thing that I got out of it was that I should not make my life decisions based on what others want or based on what others try to persuade me to do. My decisions should be mine and only mine, and I should do what is right for me. You helped me realize this. If I had to give someone that was having the same concerns as me advice, I would simply tell them that they should take the time to sit back and figure out what they want from life at their age, and make their decisions based on that. Will this

Self-Love

decision help or break your life plan? Once you've figured that out, the decisions should not be hard to make."

Your heavenly Father has a plan for your life—a plan for good, not for evil, a plan to give you a future and hope. Let me remind you that one of the reasons Jesus came here was for you to live life abundantly. Let me inform you, you are *not* alone. The Father cares for you, and you must get to know Him by praying and studying His Word. The Word of God will be a lamp unto your feet; it will illuminate your way out of dark times. I know that if He did it for me, He will do it for you, His child. But let's pause and let me ask you: Are you His child? Have you been born again? Why do I pause and ask this? Because of James 5:16 (ESV): "Therefore, confess your sins to one another and pray for one another, that you may be healed. The prayer of a righteous person has great power as it is working."

I only know of one way to have my prayers answered, and that is to be righteous. Furthermore, I only know one way to be righteous, and it is as Jesus says in John 14:6 (ESV):

"Jesus said to him, 'I am the way, and the truth, and the life. No one comes to the Father except through me.'"

Now, how do you come to Jesus? Romans 10:9 (ESV) says, "Because, if you confess with your mouth that Jesus is Lord and believe in your heart that God raised him from the dead, you will be saved."

If you desire for Jesus to come into your life, or if you just want to make sure you are saved according to the Bible, I invite you to repeat this prayer with your whole heart: "Heavenly Father, I come to You in the name of

Teach Me What Mama Didn't Know

Jesus. Thank You, Father, for loving and giving me this opportunity to confess my sins and ask You to come into my heart. I believe Jesus is Lord and that You raised Him from the dead. Lord, cleanse me from all unrighteousness. Help me to start my life over with You as my Lord and Savior. By faith, I will walk. Thank You for Your grace and mercy over my life. In Jesus's name, I pray. Amen!"

God made you exactly how He needed you to be to fit into His master plan. His plan is not a selfish plan. Yes, He will get the glory, but He desires that you, His child, have life and have it abundantly. The evilness of this world may have tried to steal your identity. Nonetheless, you are a child of the King; straighten your crown and act like it. Your heavenly Father does not desire for you to be stressed by the messed-up idea of what people think you should be. Realize that you are who God says you are. You are not to fit into the forever-changing idea of what humankind finds acceptable or unacceptable.

Note: Please master the "Self-Love" section before moving on. Declare, "Enough is enough!" If you find this challenging, ask the Holy Spirit to help you completely love the you that God created you to be. Collectively, we, you, and I are the body of Christ, and we, your true brothers and sisters in Christ, need you to survive. Parents, guardians, mentors, friends, and loved ones, sometimes talking about self-love is as hard as talking

> **MASTER THE 'SELF-LOVE' SECTION BEFORE MOVING ON**
>
> #TMWMDK

Self-Love

about funeral arrangements. To open the dialogue, it is important that you share this section with the people in your life you love and care for.

Three Verses to Look Up and Personalize:

1) Jeremiah 1:6–8

2) Philippians 4:6

3) Psalm 16:11

Speak into the Atmosphere Prayer

"Father God, thank You for teaching me how to love myself. Thank You that I no longer accept the definition of my life's worth as described by humankind. I am Yours, and You have created me as new and whole to stand strong and bold. I lift all my past uncertainties to You, fully accepting I can do all things through Christ, who strengthens me. I will no longer let the words of my mouth defeat my mind. I will, from this day forth, speak life and not death, not only over myself but also over those You place in my path. Let Your good and perfect will be done in my life. In Jesus's name. Amen."

Friends, Family, and Them

Proverbs 18:24 (ESV)

Who Are They?

A man of many companions may come to ruin, but
there is a friend who sticks closer than a brother.
—Proverbs 18:24 (ESV)

His name is Jesus! As I sit here and think about this topic of friends, family, and them, so many songs come to my mind: "What a Friend We Have in Jesus" by the Winans; "I Got Jesus and That's Enough" by the Canton Spirituals; "Forever Reign" by Hillsong Live; "For My Good" by Tamela Mann; and "The Love of Jesus" by Elevation Worship.

"Love" by Kirk Franklin

The nights that I've cried you loved me
When I should have died you loved me
I'll never know why you love me

Teach Me What Mama Didn't Know

In my adulthood, I went through a personal storm for a little over a year. Like the biblical story of the woman with the issue of blood, not one doctor could tell me what was going on. Like Job from the Bible, not one friend could give me the right comforting words. Like King David, not one family member could console the deep crying in my soul. But Jesus, my friend and wonderful counselor, He walked with me and talked with me and assured me that I was His own. When no one could help me, Jesus did, each and every time. He is indeed that friend who sticks closer than a sister or a brother.

You will notice that I use the word *friend* more than I use the word *family*, and here is why. If you are old enough to read this book, I am sure by now you have heard the saying, "Blood doesn't make you family." Let's put it another way: blood makes you related; loyalty makes you family. This simply means that sometimes the loyalty of friends is greater and more dependable than that of blood-related family.

My grandmother Frances once said to me, "You finally got the family you always wanted." She was speaking of my in-laws. My grandmother knew the emotional pain I dealt with as a kid, just trying to fit in with some of my own blood-related family members. That blood bond didn't manifest until I was good and grown. In the meantime, my husband and a select few of his relatives loved me as if I were their own.

Speaking of my husband, he's witnessed on-and-off relationships I've had with friends and family through the years; lukewarm or cold relationships are not acceptable

Friends, Family, and Them

to me. I do not like drama or games being played with my emotions. Early on, I adopted the mind-set of *either you want to be a part of my life or you don't*. If you do not, I am okay with that. So the moment a person shows any signs of being lukewarm toward me, I begin the process of letting them go.

I have friends who refuse to write me off, no matter how many times I tell them they are getting on my last nerve. They've known me long enough and understand my no-nonsense personality. We therefore communicate and begin quickly restoring what's broken between us. Why? Because our constant display of loyalty toward one another through the years has made us family.

Friends come, and friends go, and the same is true for family. This is one reason why it's extremely important you learn to love yourself! Because if you don't love yourself first, those, who like rotating doors, come in and out of your life, can cause you to unnecessarily be depressed, stressed, and angry.

Let's pause to define the "Them" found in the title of this section. It refers to those who flat-out don't like you, those who pretend to like you for their own personal gain, and those you try to please, hoping to be accepted by them.

Who Are You?

If you, in trying to please others, change who you are meant to be, then you will always feel like you are having the worst life ever, when you are supposed to experience the best life ever. Everyone must find his or her own purpose in this life. People can cause you to lose sight of your purpose and the greatness you are destined for. So the question is, Who are you?

> EVERYONE MUST FIND HIS OR HER OWN PURPOSE IN THIS LIFE
>
>
>
> #TMWMDK

Some people might see that you're good at cooking, so they'll try to persuade you to be a chef. Some might see that you're good at computers, so they'll try to persuade you to work in the technology field. Some might see you're good at speaking, that you have a kind heart, and that you love the Lord, so they might try to persuade you to be a preacher. Some people will notice your natural athletic abilities and try to force you to travel the path toward stardom in the athletic world. Some people, living with their own regrets, will try to make you into what they should've been. Some will try to persuade you to follow in your parents' footsteps. And

Friends, Family, and Them

some are absolutely not going to believe in the hopes and dreams you have for yourself. So again, the question is, Who are you? Now, you may have never thought about this. You may have no idea what you want to do, but I guarantee you God knows what He created you to be. And trust me—His plan is not to give you some boring, dreadful life. Jeremiah 29:11 (ESV) says, "For I know the plans I have for you, declares the Lord, plans for peace and not for evil, to give you a future and a hope."

I pray that, in reading this book, you awaken to the truth that you are designed to succeed. I pray that you realize you can have a great, prosperous life. I pray that you recognize the truth as laid out in the Bible: God personally knows who you are. God has plans to give you hope and a future. He knows what's best for the uniqueness in you.

Imagine your favorite flower, your favorite meal, and your favorite music. If every flower looked and smelled the same, if everything you ate tasted the same, and every beat to your favorite tune was the same, where would the joy of something new spring from? There are almost ten thousand different species of birds. Almost six hundred thousand different types of flowers bring fragrances and beauty to this world. And over seven billion people are alive, occupying this home we call earth. Of the seven billion people, one of them is you.

Take a moment and visualize it; you are one out of seven billion. You are fearfully and wonderfully made by the Master Craftsman, Yahweh-Bore, God the Creator. Just like you are in awe when you see different kinds of awesome things you like, God is in awe when He sees you. He loves you! So be the you He created you to be, not the you someone else is trying to turn you into. Caterpillars turn into butterflies, not frogs. Don't let others turn you into something you are not meant to be. Also, if you are unsure of your place in this world and would like to succeed in your dreams and goals, you must be willing to seek out and listen to the advice of established leaders and those in your community who are wise.

Special Note

In a world full of peer pressure and easily accessible self-defeating ideas, it is a must that we have patience with the younger generation when proactively helping them figure out their place in this world. The Bible tells us to be kind and compassionate with one another. We must maintain a kind and compassionate mind frame when providing guidance. This means, when you don't understand the mind-set of someone you care for, instead of becoming annoyed, take the time to step away and pray. In your prayer, ask God to give you the right words to say. Continue to maintain a heart of hope and that trust in the end, He will make all things right.

They Can Hurt You

In writing this book, one thing I purposed not to do was put names to those who abused me as a kid. It is because I am a firm believer in Matthew 7:12 (ESV): "So whatever you wish that others would do to you, do also to them, for this is the Law and the Prophets."

If I did something to someone and they have forgiven me, I wouldn't want them to keep bringing the matter up every time they saw me. Constantly attaching a name to an issue or an issue to a person suggests we haven't truly forgiven them, and the wounds of the past never fully heal. Those who caused harm to me know what they have done. Even though some of them have not asked me to, I have forgiven them because it frees me to live a full, abundant life. If they haven't forgiven themselves, that's between them and God.

Perhaps at this point in your life, you have people who have hurt you deeply. You may have been abused—physically, spiritually, sexually, mentally, verbally, or emotionally. Perhaps you, like I, have experienced all of these forms of abuse. Yes, I have been there. I know what it's like to feel like you are all alone in this world, and to feel like those who are supposed to protect you are the ones causing you distress. Trust me when I say life will not become worth living until you let go of the hurts from your past.

You can become a Christian, you can read your Bible, and you can attend every church service. But there is a thing called forgiving and forgetting. When you mature in Christ, you will discover that forgiving is easy. The brain, however, doesn't so easily forget. Still, to fully live a free life, you must choose to forget. How? By never bringing the matter up to the person who harmed you after you have forgiven them.

Though I have forgiven those who treated me wrong, I share this next bit of information with the prayer that it will help someone reading this to end the silence. I was in seventh grade when I realized that having my private parts touched and being made to perform sexual acts was inappropriate behavior. Some of you may wonder why it took me so long to know that this behavior was wrong. Well, when the behavior starts when you're a toddler, the acts are being taught to you by adults, there are multiple people involved, and there is not a responsible adult around to sense something is wrong, you can go a long time before the light bulb comes on. So if you are being made to perform sexual acts, whether it is from an adult, a friend, a family member, the family of a friend, or a kid, please tell someone.

PLEASE TELL SOMEONE

#TMWMDK

Everywhere I go, when I hear kids say to each other, "Let's play house," I cringe! The red flag alert goes into full effect, and my response is "You

Friends, Family, and Them

better get somewhere and play church!" Another thing that causes me to cringe is hearing kids say they are about to play hide-and-seek. When I was a child, hide-and-seek was a code word for hide and go get it, which meant I was about to be violated again. I understand that some youth playing hide and go get it were never sexually abused. It was their hormones that got them excited to play such a game. But having a history of being violated, hide-and-seek was not a game I wanted to play. And having adults taunt me and call me weird and standoffish while forcing me to go play with the other neighborhood kids made matters even worse.

I remember as a kid being threatened with death by some of my abusers. I also remember being bribed with something as simple as bubble gum to do some of the most ungodly things. If you are a kid and someone is threatening you or trying to bribe you into doing wrongful acts, I am praying that you find the courage to make them stop. Tell your mom, tell your dad, tell your grandparents, tell anyone in your family who you feel is bigger and stronger than the person who is abusing or threatening you. Please don't believe the lie from Satan of "You don't want to get that person in trouble." Satan is using that person to try to destroy your future.

> **PLEASE DON'T BELIEVE THE LIE FROM SATAN**
>
> #TMWMDK

Parents, guardians, mentors, friends, and loved ones, it is very important to research and know the signs that a child has been sexually abused. Some of them are as follows:

- The child displays inappropriate sexual behaviors toward themselves and others. This can be a critical, sensitive moment in a child's life.
    - Correct the child, but here's why you should not be harsh:
        - 1) Children typically imitate what they have learned.
        - 2) Because the child can shut down and you can miss the opportunity to effectively communicate with them and discover that they learned this behavior by being handled inappropriately.
    - Determine how big the problem might be, and seek outside professional counseling for the child as necessary.
- The child has a sudden change of mood—for example, instantly shy or standoffish.
- The child is adamant about not wanting to be left alone with certain people.

Because adults had sexually abused me as a kid, when I became an adult, I was very leery of adults who went secretively missing while they were engaging in activities with children. I am easily frustrated with adults who don't seem to have boundaries when it comes to being in a child's personal space. Also, adults who are always eager to volunteer and take kids on fun dates alone cause me to be on high alert.

Abuse is a complicated mess. Physically, spiritually, sexually, mentally, verbally, and emotionally abused

Friends, Family, and Them

people can sometimes abuse other people. For it is true: hurt people hurt other people, just like bullies. However, understand that if you are a person who has been abused, I am a witness to the fact that you can end the cycle. Instead of hurting others, you can be the hurt person who heals other people, just like I am doing. Totally surrender to the healing power of Jesus. Forgive yourself, ask for forgiveness, and help others to heal by forgiving them.

Anyone in the category of "friends, family, and them" can purposely hurt you. Why? Because of the evilness of human nature. It is my prayer that informing you of this will cause you to be determined to live your God-given unique life. If you are being abused, speak up. Don't stay silent. Tell someone in your family you trust. Had I been advised to tell someone, I would have told my great-grandmother much sooner than I did. As soon as I told her, she did something about it, and the abuse began to stop.

Every child has big dreams of one day doing great things. You are designed for greatness. Do not remain silent; don't be robbed of your greatness. Just as you would tell an adult if someone tried to rob you of your lunch or bicycle, tell an adult if someone tries to rob you of your greatness by physically, spiritually, sexually, mentally, verbally, or emotionally abusing you.

Consequences

Growing up, I moved back and forth from state to state, so I have friends, but I don't have lifelong friends. Watching my kids grow up in the same area, I realize there are age levels of friendships. Most friends you start with in elementary school don't acknowledge your existence by the time you get into high school. Most ties between high school friends are lost right after graduation. Those lost friendships do not mean something is wrong with you or the other person. Ecclesiastes chapter 3 lets us know there is a time and season for everything. Not only do time and distance separate people, but people often outgrow one another. It's the way life goes. Most childhood friendships are temporary. Those friendships expire; they are not meant to last forever. With that said, do not let foolish decisions for temporary friends cause you to miss out on your greatness.

Seriously go over the following table:

Foolish Decisions Made for Temporary Friends	Some of the Consequences You Might Face

Friends, Family, and Them

Doing drugs and underage drinking	Death, jail, or possibly killing or causing bodily harm to others. Prematurely aging skin and internal body organs. Living with a life full of regrets.
Having sex before marriage	Pregnancy, with lifelong baby mama or baby daddy issues. Lifelong sexually transmitted disease(s). Living with a life full of regrets.
Stealing	Jail. Killing or causing someone to lose their life. Living with a life full of regrets.
Rebelling and lying about your age	Being permanently labeled as a liar. Missing out on great opportunities that could help you achieve your goals. Being placed in danger and causing others to be jailed or harmed. Living with a life full of regrets.
Being mean, strongly joking about the shortcomings of others	Causing someone to do bodily harm to themselves, you, or others. Missing opportunities that could brighten your future. Living with a life full of regrets.

| Following the dreams and goals of friends and others, and following the advice of foolish people | Missing out on opportunities. Always feeling empty, unsatisfied, and unaccomplished. Living with a life full of regrets. |

Out loud, make the above personal by saying: "If I am (insert the decision), then I can end up (insert the consequence)." Repeat for each of the decisions and consequences.

Are you okay with those consequences, making life harder than it's supposed to be? Some people will call it karma; the Bible calls it sowing and reaping. Galatians 6:7 (ESV) says, "Do not be deceived: God is not mocked, for whatever one sows, that will he also reap."

MAKING LIFE HARDER THAN IT'S SUPPOSED TO BE

#TMWMDK

This world can be a lonely, hard place. There are people who purposely make life hard for others. Please don't make life hard for yourself!

Dream Killers

We've talked about how people can cause you to lose sight of your purpose. Clearly understand that if you're not careful, Satan will use you to be a dream killer as well. Keep your guard up by studying the Bible to know wrong from right, and ask the Holy Spirit to be your guiding light. Please don't let yourself be used as a dream killer, killing not only the dreams of others but your own dreams as well. In John 10:10 (ESV), Jesus says, "The thief comes only to steal and kill and destroy. I came that they may have life and have it abundantly."

Perhaps you are wondering, who is the thief? The thief is anyone who has let their Christian guard down. Let me explain. Some people are looking for signs of the devil. They are expecting him as a spirit roaming, and they fail to realize the devil can use people. He can use the sweetest kid down the street, the teacher, the preacher, friends, and family. Satan can use them to destroy your visions and your goals. If you are not careful, he can use you to be a dream killer, destroying the hopes and plans God has for someone else's life. Gossip, lies, slander, rumors, and mindlessly pointing out someone else's behaviors that are contrary to yours are ways Satan can use you. Even in reading the prior sentence, you may not have acknowledged the fact that you could possibly be one of Satan's puppets. Gossip, lies, and so on are not of God. So ask yourself, Have I been known to laugh and gossip about someone's behavior that is contrary to my own? Have I been quick to clearly see and point out what others are not doing right?

In mentioning dream killers, two scriptures come to mind. The first one is Matthew 7:1 (ESV): "Judge not, that you be not judged." The second one is Matthew 7:5 (ESV): "You hypocrite, first take the log out of your own eye, and then you will see clearly to take the speck out of your brother's eye."

Again, don't be a dream killer. Life can be a harsh, lonely place all by itself. Find the best words to encourage others to do the right thing. Yes, you may have the gift to clearly see a person going down a path of destruction. Use the gift for good by praying to the Lord on the person's behalf. Take caution to make sure you are not being like the Pharisee from the biblical parable of the Pharisee and the tax collector in Luke 18:10–14 (ESV):

> Two men went up into the temple to pray, one a Pharisee and the other a tax collector. The Pharisee, standing by himself, prayed thus: "God, I thank you that I am not like other men, extortioners, unjust, adulterers, or even like this tax collector. I fast twice a week; I give tithes

> of all that I get." But the tax collector, standing far off, would not even lift up his eyes to heaven, but beat his breast, saying, "God, be merciful to me, a sinner!" I tell you, this man went down to his house justified, rather than the other. For everyone who exalts himself will be humbled, but the one who humbles himself will be exalted.

Sometimes we get so deep in our self-religious ideas we use the Bible's words and ideas word for word. We forget we may need to apply it to our own situation. So let's clear some things up. Like the Pharisee, you may not be pointing out the fact that people are extortioners, unjust, and adulterers. Perhaps instead you are negatively discussing with others the way someone is dressed, with clothing too revealing or pants sagging. Perhaps you are gossiping about the fact that someone is pregnant, while forgetting you are participating in making out. By the way, making out is the step that leads to sex, which leads to getting pregnant.

There are so many things you can point out about the misbehaviors of others. I am in no way condoning the behaviors of others. However, clearly understand that our heavenly Father works in mysterious ways. His thoughts are not our thoughts, and His ways are definitely not our ways. He can use mishaps for His glory. Be kind and compassionate. Pray for others to be made whole. Encourage them to walk in their God-ordained purpose.

You never know how God may be using someone. He used a prostitute to clean the feet of Jesus. Furthermore, there were plenty of religious people who did not understand our Lord and Savior, Jesus the Christ. Pray for those whose lifestyle you don't understand or agree with. No matter how young or how old you are, I'm sure there is someone out in this world still praying for you to be who God created you to be. So be an encourager, thinking positively and sincerely pray for those who are doing things contrary to the Word of God.

This is an ever-evolving world. Always remember to have fun and enjoy your life. Do not let your dreams be killed, and do not become a dream killer. Just as you change, other people change too. Friends, family, and others will come and go. Be who you are designed to be.

REMEMBER TO HAVE FUN AND ENJOY YOUR LIFE

#TMWMDK

As you are finding your unique self, the person God created you to be, remember to let other people be who God created them to be. Do not judge and do not falsely accuse. We all have our shortcomings. Just as you would want someone to encourage you to be better with love and kind words, remember to be an encourager.

Special Note

Do not let past hurts cause you to become an abuser, a predator, or anything else that is against the Word of God. When you get to heaven, God will not accept past

Friends, Family, and Them

hurts as an excuse for your choice of behaviors. While you are still here on earth, God can heal you. He can make you whole; you must, however, turn it all over to Him. Seek counseling if necessary. Again, as said in the Bible, the enemy comes to steal, kill, and destroy, but Jesus came so you can have life and have it abundantly. Also, if you were taught to perform sexual acts as a kid, forgive yourself. Kids do what they learn. If you feel the other person was affected by the behavior, forgive them. Ask for forgiveness, and both of you seek counseling together if necessary. Parents, guardians, mentors, friends, and loved ones, sometimes talking about abuse is as hard as talking about funeral arrangements. To open the dialogue, it is important that you share these chapters with the children and people in your life who you love and care about.

Three Verses to Look Up and Personalize:

1) Ecclesiastes 4:12

2) Ephesians 4:32

3) 1 John 4:7–8

Teach Me What Mama Didn't Know

Speak into the Atmosphere Prayer

"Father God, thank You for teaching me that though friends, family, and others will fail me, You will always remain my true help in this life. I thank You for healing the wounds of my past. Lord, I thank You for loving me and having plans to give me hope and a future. Thank You for desiring that I have life abundantly. I thank You that brighter days are ahead. I thank You for placing me on a path to heal others. Thank You for helping me to forgive others as I so desire You to forgive me. In Jesus's name, I pray. Amen."

Fleeing Temptation

James 4:7 (ESV)

Keep the Lord's Covenant

Submit yourselves therefore to God. Resist
the devil, and he will flee from you.
—James 4:7 (ESV)

Don't chase the man; chase God. The man will come. Don't chase the woman; chase God. The woman will come. For me to be interested in dating someone, he had to be extremely intelligent first and good-looking second. I know that may seem obvious, but it's not. Some people are only interested in how much money a person has; they are not as interested in the person's intellect. There are plenty of other things a person goes by to choose their mate. Intellect is one of the reasons I am head over heels for my husband. That handsome, strong, compassionate man is *Jeopardy* and *Who Wants to Be a Millionaire?*–winning kind of smart.

However, before my husband came along, I at one point found myself in rotating relationships, like people showing up for an interview. Next ... Next ... Next. Eventually, at a young age, I got bored and frustrated with the dating scene. Ironically, during my years of dating, when I didn't have self-love, I still knew what type of mate I wanted to have, thanks to the *Cosby Show* and the marriage of my aunt Beverly and uncle Willie. They were wonderful examples of what a family should be like. Outside of that, growing up, I didn't have much of an example of how a husband and wife with children should operate. It may seem strange, but when I got married, I didn't know the purpose of marriage. I figured it was something you were supposed to do or something that was nice to do. I didn't know marriage took more than love, that it also takes work, patience, and humility. I now know marriage was biblically designed by God, and it is His desire that the two, man and woman, should come together as husband and wife. Marriage in God's eyes is an example of His love and covenant to the church. Because of my goal to honor God's desire, I have enjoyed having someone to share everyday life with. I have also enjoyed having my husband there to support me through difficult times. I am also enjoying having someone to raise children with while building lifelong legacies together.

Now back to my bored and frustrated dating years. I can remember being so fed up with dating, I got down

Fleeing Temptation

on my knees and prayed to God. I said, "Lord, I'm tired of dating, I'm tired of the games, I'm tired of wasting my time. God, if You want me to be with someone, You are going to have to do this, because as long as I am conscious, everyone who approaches me is going to get a loud, resounding, 'No!'" I think that prayer took off in the atmosphere and did something supernatural, because when my husband came along, he swears I was sweating him from the start. Lord knows, our union has had its share of bumps and bruises. Nonetheless, God couldn't have picked a better mate for me. Yes, I say this even though, jokingly, the man has the nerve to tell everyone who will listen, "I turned her into a woman."

Was my husband the first person I dated? No. Was he the second? No. He was not the third, fourth, or the fifth. Again, it didn't take much for me to quickly become uninterested in someone. I remember one guy became good friends with my dad. And that was the end of our relationship. I was like "No. If you have become friends with my dad, I will no longer date you." You'd have to know my dad to understand why. Yes, my dad was cool, and he was smooth, but no, not happening. Being from Detroit, Michigan, I remember ending a relationship with a guy because he pretended to have a gun. It's one thing to have a gun. It's another thing to make jesters in public to suggest you have one; fool around and get us both shot. *No. Bye.* Oh, and then there was the married one. Yes, the married one! No, I did not know he was married until his wife called. She wanted to know why I was answering her husband's phone. Well, shoot, I wanted to know the same thing. So I gathered my thoughts and asked him in my cool, calm, and collected way, "Um, so you have a wife?" He begrudgingly informed me that they were separated and about to get a divorce. Needless to say, I left him quickly.

Now, please hear me out. If someone you are interested in tells you they are separated but not divorced, walk away. Better yet, run! First, please don't sign up for dealing with the temptation that comes with the act of adultery. In God's eyes, the two are still one. Second, I have seen plenty of people get hurt because they believed their supposed partner was going to leave their spouse. Third, it doesn't always happen the way you wish. I know this from experience. Somewhere between year six and seven of my marriage, my husband and I separated with the goal to be divorced. However, with the desire to keep the Lord's covenant example, and having been taught from Him that we are not each other's enemies, that Satan is the real enemy, we are still married and growing stronger together every day.

Declare Purity

I might as well be transparent and keep it real. I mentioned that my husband was not the first person I dated. He was also not the first person I willingly had intercourse with. I am in no way suggesting sex before marriage. I have now been taught by our heavenly Father that it's definitely best to flee the temptation of fornication and to declare purity by sustaining from sexual immorality, as stated in 1 Thessalonians 4:3–5 (ESV): "For this is the will of God, your sanctification: that you abstain from sexual immorality; that each one of you know how to control his own body in holiness and honor, not in the passion of lust like the Gentiles who do not know God."

Moving along, this was my initial logic for having sex before I got married: because of the sexual abuse I endured as a child, I had, in my mind, concluded I was not a virgin. Why? Because my virginity was taken from me well before I knew what being a virgin meant. So by the time I realized the meaning of being a virgin, because of the sexual acts I was made to perform as a child, I was already past the virgin point. Nothing else mattered, so I thought. See, no one at that time came to me and told me how unique and precious I was. Nor did they tell me

Teach Me What Mama Didn't Know

to preserve my goods for someone worthy. The talks I got about sex went something like this: "You get pregnant, I'm going to kill you." Not even thinking about being killed, my mind was mainly stuck on the word *pregnant*. I thought, *If I was molested numerous times and didn't get pregnant, just how does one actually get pregnant?* I had never been taught sex education. I share this information because I want those of you who have been abused to not adopt the mind-set I had. Respect your body. Protect your goods. Had I been taught differently then, I would have done things differently. I would have fled the temptation of fornication.

I know I am not alone with the virginity thought process I had. I've counseled sexually abused people who informed me they too once questioned the whole virginity concept. If you are a victim of sexual abuse, look at it this way: if someone slaps you, it doesn't mean you go around willingly saying, "Well, I've been slapped before, so here—slap me again and again." No! Just as with sexual abuse, don't go around saying, "Well, I've been sexually abused, so here—you can have my body—and you over there, you can have my body too." I am encouraging you to reclaim what was wrongfully stolen from you—your identity, your pureness, your wholeness. I am encouraging you to be transformed by the renewing of your mind. Declare you will no longer be a victim of the abusive choices made by others. Again, I say, respect your

> RECLAIM WHAT WAS WRONGFULLY STOLEN FROM YOU
>
>
>
> #TMWMDK

Fleeing Temptation

body. Protect your goods. Just because you are a male, having been molested by men doesn't mean you have to stay trapped by the idea of loving other men. Same goes for females. Just because you were taught to do some of the most dreadful things doesn't mean you have to stay trapped by Satan's snares. Who the Son sets free is free indeed. I know plenty of people who have reclaimed their identity as designed by Christ. I sit here and raise my hand, for I am a witness. I wanted the normalcy of pureness and wholeness as He designed me. I studied God's Word, I got to know Jesus, I fell in love with Him, and He changed my life for my good and for His Glory.

If it wasn't for the grace and mercy of God, I don't even want to imagine where I would be. God kept me. He didn't let me drown in the life choices Satan tried to make for me. God is ready to keep you! He will fix for you whatever is causing you to fall into the temptation of doing things contrary to His Word. You must, however, lean not on your own understanding. Totally surrender all and trust Him. You must let go and let God rewrite the script.

Be Steadfast

Though there is a section on marriage, let's discuss marriage and temptation. I remember receiving two pieces of advice pertaining to marriage. One was "Why buy the cow when he can get the milk for free?" I'm still trying to figure out how that statement relates to me and my question of "Should I get married?" The second was "Go ahead and get married. You can always get a divorce." Hmm. Well, let's look at marriage from the Bible standpoint, focusing on four scriptures.

The first scripture deals with fornication: "Flee from sexual immorality. Every other sin a person commits is outside the body, but the sexually immoral person sins against his own body. Or do you not know that your body is a temple of the Holy Spirit within you, whom you have from God? You are not your own" (1 Corinthians 6:18–19 ESV).

The second scripture deals with the question of *to be single or not to be*: "To the unmarried and the widows I say that it is good for them to remain single, as I am. But if they cannot exercise self-control, they should marry. For it is better to marry than to burn with passion" (1 Corinthians 7:8–9 ESV).

Fleeing Temptation

The third scripture deals with being married: "Therefore a man shall leave his father and his mother and hold fast to his wife, and they shall become one flesh" (Genesis 2:24 ESV).

The fourth scripture deals with divorce: "For the man who does not love his wife but divorces her, says the LORD, the God of Israel, covers his garment with violence, says the LORD of hosts. So guard yourselves in your spirit, and do not be faithless" (Malachi 2:16 ESV).

Above all, I aim to please the Lord. He is indeed my first true love. There are times I think, if I was single, I could be free to do so much for the kingdom of God. However, I know sin would always be knocking at my door. Sin would tempt me by demanding I be a fornicating, sexual, immoral person, so, in agreement with the Word of God, it's best that I am married. And since I am married, I must do my part to ensure I am as one with my husband.

I often meet people who want to know the secret to my long-lasting marriage. Of course, I immediately purposely kill the thought they have of everything being perfect between my husband and me. I go on and tell them that, above everything, Daniel and I put God first. Yes, he puts God before me, and I put God before him. Doing this holds us directly responsible to God for our actions on an individual level. I also tell them he and I have declared to one another, our children, and to anyone whom will listen that just as he and I chose to be husband and wife, we also choose to be best friends. I tell them, "Just as in your loyal relationships with your best friends, your siblings, your parents, and your cousins, your spouse will never be as God—perfect in all His ways." So you must learn to pick your battles and take *every* situation to the Lord in prayer.

Even though God is our solid rock, we accept that we are two imperfect best friends. Because of various tests, trials, tribulations, and temptations, we sometimes have to put each other in temporary time-out. We refuse to give up on each other. Why? Because on an individual level, we love God. Saying we love God is not something we just sing or preach about from the pulpit. Again, above everything, we desire to do what is pleasing in the Lord's sight. This includes resisting the devil, fleeing temptation, and believing wholeheartedly that God has something better for us—something much better than the simple, temporary fixes that temptations try to provide.

Daniel and I have been together a long time. Our time together has been well worth every second, minute, hour, day, and year, but it hasn't always been easy. To this day, from time to time, there are disagreements in our marriage. I can recall in one of our disagreements being strongly tempted to end my marriage. During that time, the Holy Spirit constantly reminded me of God's example of unfailing love. I was being confrontational, saying to the Holy Spirit, "You've got to be kidding me, right?" However, I found myself praying, "Lord, nothing in my flesh wants to say this prayer, but that little ray of light, deep down at the very bottom of my spirit, is

Fleeing Temptation

crying out for help. So, Lord, help me do what's pleasing in Your sight." And the Lord did, though I put up a fight.

Since I'm a Christian, you may find yourself judging me as I'm being openly transparent and honest with you. But let me help you quickly get back on track by sharing a Bible verse with you, John 8:7 (ESV): "And as they continued to ask him, he stood up and said to them, 'Let him who is without sin among you be the first to throw a stone at her.'"

There, you have it. Now let's refocus. I share this bit about what I personally dealt with to let you know you are not alone when dealing with temptation. I know temptation is real, but I also know, through experience, you can flee temptation.

YOU ARE NOT ALONE

#TMWMDK

You won't find many adults who will be honest and tell you the real temptations they wrestle with in their day-to-day personal lives. They may point out the funny, less harmful temptations they deal with. But rarely will someone let you know his or her struggle is real. I have discovered that oftentimes adults paint illusions of a picture-perfect life. This illusion has caused children to struggle unnecessarily when they reach adulthood. They stress over trying to achieve for themselves a perfect life. But hear me clearly: there is no such thing as a flawless, perfect life. All adults commonly deal with stressful situations, temptations, tests, trials, and tribulations. So no matter what test, trial, or temptation you are struggling with in your life, you are not alone. Yet this is not an excuse. And saying words like "God knows my heart" does not work when it comes to obeying the Word of God. You must find a solid ground to stand on and be steadfast.

As for marriage, know this: just like any relationship, it comes with joys and sorrows, good days and bad days, ups and downs. This is why it's important to marry someone you absolutely love. Never marry for convenience or just for the sake of saying you're married; doing so will definitely cause unnecessary stress. Furthermore, tests, trials, tribulations, and temptations will come in many forms. It is important to know that just because your marriage may one day be presented with its own set of difficulties, it doesn't mean something is wrong with you, nor does it mean something is wrong with your spouse. It's okay to disagree from time to time; just remember to never become disagreeable. What I suggest is starting early, before problems occur, earnestly praying and attending worship services together. God can help you lovingly stay together. And contrary to what some will have you believe, there is absolutely nothing wrong with seeking counseling on an individual level and together.

80 - 18 = 62

Now to elaborate on chasing God and not the person, as mentioned earlier. The Bible lets us know in several verses that God is a jealous God. We are to not have any other god before Him. Sometimes in looking for a mate, you may find yourself tempted to put God on the back burner (making Him your lowest priority). You do this by ignoring what God says about fornication (1 Thessalonians 4:3–5) or ignoring what God says about adultery (Hebrews 13:4).

Therefore, by engaging in adultery or fornication (whether first base, as some call "making out," or home base, "all in"), if you are trying to get a mate by submitting to the voice of temptation, you are indeed placing that person before God. When we choose to ignore the commands of God, we, like Adam and Eve, choose to invite unknown, unnecessary destruction into our lives.

We have thus far spoken on the temptations of being in a relationship, especially my own desire to flee temptation. Trust me when I say it wasn't always easy. There was definitely a struggle within me between two desires—the will to do wrong and the will to do right.

Teach Me What Mama Didn't Know

At times, Satan tried to misquote scripture to me. He took several different angles, attempting to make me go against what I knew was right according to the Word of God. Based on my temporary feelings and emotions, he tried to use me to fix scripture according to my liking. I often found myself mumbling the words "Lord, help me to stand fully committed to Your will, Your ways, and Your Word." I fought temptation. How did I fight? By resisting the devil. How did I resist the devil? By removing myself from the temporary feelings attached to temporary situations. I fought by crying out to the one person who wins every battle. I cried out to the Lord!

As for your temptations, you may not be fighting against fornication or adultery. However, as sin is sin, temptation is temptation. If you truly love the Lord, you must be willing to ask Him to help you resist the devil's suggestions. It does not matter if you are fighting the temptations of sexual immorality, stealing, being mean and hateful, desiring to kill, lying, cheating, dishonoring your parents or authority, drugs, alcoholism, gluttony; whatever your temptation is, it can be conquered.

Because I truly love the Lord, I cried out to Him for help. Believe me when I say I felt like a person at the brink of fainting, crying out to God with my last breath, "Lord ... help ... me." If you are struggling with doing the right thing by God, I ask you, Do you really love the Lord? Or is at just a familiar song you sing? Do the words "I love God" easily come from your mouth with no true meaning? If you really love the Lord, sincerely, with your whole heart, ask Him to help you. He will

Fleeing Temptation

help you because He truly loves and cares for you, more than anyone else does. The Bible tells us in James 4:7 (ESV) that the way to evade temptation is to "Submit yourselves therefore to God. Resist the devil, and he will flee from you."

In 1 John 5:3 (ESV), it says, "For this is the love of God, that we keep his commandments. And his commandments are not burdensome."

John 14:15 (ESV) says, "If you love me, you will keep my commandments."

So again, the question is, Do you really love the Lord? Or is it just a song you sing? Do you find the commandments of the Lord to be burdensome, or will you lean not unto your own understanding and trust Him? Trust He has plans to give you an abundant life, and trust He knows what's best for you. I have come to witness that if you do things as God has said in His Word, He will not only keep you in perfect peace but give you your real heart's desire. You don't have to do the wrong things to receive good things. Doing things God's way definitely leads to less stress, fewer restless nights, less depression, and fewer regrets.

The "Self-Love" and "Friends, Family, and Them" chapters discussed some of the wrongdoings of others toward you that can cause you to live a downward-spiraling life, but only if you let it. This section, "Fleeing Temptation," has been written to awaken you to the reality that the average person lives their first eighteen years under the rules, ideas, and decisions of someone else. The average person may live to see his or her eightieth birthday. In doing the math, 80 − 18 = 62. You get sixty-two years of choices, far more than the choices someone made for you in your first eighteen years.

What people do to you only lasts a season, but the consequences of what you do to yourself can last a lifetime. Temptation is not a physical battle. Temptation is a spiritual battle. That battle starts in the mind. Resist the devil, and he will flee. Resist by getting up. Occupy your mind with something else, start praying, start singing, or call a friend. Start trusting and believing that, yes, you deserve better—better than temporary false fixes provided by temptation's lies.

> WHAT PEOPLE DO TO YOU ONLY LASTS A SEASON
>
>
>
> #TMWMDK

According to Proverbs 14:12 (ESV), "There is a way that seems right to a man, but its end is the way to death." Following the voice of temptation, you will surely die. You may be wondering, *How will I die from lying to someone? How will I die from cheating someone? How will I die if I'm always rude and mean to someone? How will I die from sexual immorality? How will I die if it's just pleasing me and not hurting anyone else? How will I die [enter your temptation here]?* I'm sure Satan had Adam and Eve wondering the same thing, and we are all still suffering from the consequences of their decisions. The more you yield to the suggestions of temptation, you will die by being separated from God and the many blessings He has for you. There is a saying that goes something like this: "When you give the devil an inch, he will take a mile." This basically means when you give into the temptations

Fleeing Temptation

of Satan to do one thing, you open yourself up to make it easier for him to tempt you to not only do that same thing again but also do plenty of other things that are not pleasing to your heavenly Father.

This section started off by encouraging you not to chase after the man or woman but to chase God. I am here to let you know you must not chase after the things of this world either. In chasing things, we tend to fall into various temptations in order to achieve those things we feel we deserve. Don't get me wrong. I totally believe you may rightfully deserve everything your heart desires. But don't fall into temptation to get them. Your heavenly Father has a much better, less stressful way for you to enjoy an amazing life.

Think about some of the things you've already done because of the voice of temptation. What has it gotten you besides more stress, plotting more wicked schemes, and feeling more guilt without the outcome you hoped to have? How does it make you feel when others constantly do things against you and they know you don't like it? How do you think it makes your heavenly Father feel when you willingly do things not pleasing to Him?

Temptation is not just based on the things you do; sometimes it's based on the things you don't do. There is a quote that says, "Those who think they have no time for bodily exercise will sooner or later have time for illness." Remember to take care of your body. You only get one. Another quote I'm fond of says, "Never put off until tomorrow what you can do today." Sometimes later becomes never, and you find yourself struggling unnecessarily to achieve your goals. So as for fleeing temptation, whether it's fleeing from things you are doing or things you are not doing, please be strong. Don't be weak! Resist the devil, and he will flee!

Three Verses to Look Up and Personalize:

1) 1 Corinthians 10:13

2) James 4:7

3) Psalm 27:14

Speak into the Atmosphere Prayer

"Heavenly Father, thank You for teaching me to flee temptation. Thank You for teaching me the devil comes to kill, steal, and destroy but You sent Your Son that I may have life and have it abundantly. Thank You for the ability to resist the devil and no longer fall into his traps. Thank You for not giving me more than I can bear. Thank You for the Holy Spirit and the strength to stay on the path that is straight and narrow. In Jesus's name I pray. Amen."

Marriage and Parenting

Mark 10:6-9 (ESV) &
Colossians 3:21 (ESV)

How Long Should You Wait?

> Because of your hardness of heart he wrote you this commandment. But from the beginning of creation, "God made them male and female." "Therefore a man shall leave his father and mother and hold fast to his wife, and the two shall become one flesh." So they are no longer two but one flesh. What therefore God has joined together, let not man separate.
> —Mark 10:6–9 (ESV)

When discussing marriage, one of the questions many people ask is "How long should I wait before getting married?" But before we jump in on this marriage subject, let me tell you about my best friend, my husband, and the time he saved me from drowning in the Caribbean Sea. We were celebrating our tenth anniversary in the

Teach Me What Mama Didn't Know

Dominican Republic, and on this particular day, we decided to enjoy time together on the beach.

What I remember about the beach water was that it filled me with exuberance, though its waves often slapped me in the face, and its taste was extremely salty. Because of the intensity of the incoming waves, we decided to sign out life jackets and bodyboards. Upon my return to the water after retrieving my gear, there was a lady leaving the beach. She looked at her bodyboard and then looked at me and said, "This thing is not your friend!" Of course, I thought, *I got this*, and entered the water with pride. At some point, I noticed we were getting farther from the shore, but it hadn't dawned on me I might not be able to touch the bottom with my feet. At least not until my husband mentioned his feet were not touching the bottom (he's six three, and I'm five three).

When I realized he wasn't joking, I felt a slight panic and asked him to get me back to shore. As soon as he turned to put himself in a position to swim me in, a wave came, and I drifted about forty additional feet out into the water. The riptide continued to quickly pull me out farther. He asked me to swim toward him, and if you haven't figured it out by now, I didn't know how to swim. But, thanks be to God, there was a snorkeler where I drifted out to. My husband called out to the man, asking him to help me. This gentleman made great attempts, but it didn't seem as if we were going anywhere in the right direction.

I was probably a little more than three hundred feet from shore when I saw one of the hotel entertainers

Marriage and Parenting

swimming toward me. He eventually made it to where I was, grabbed me, and pulled me to my husband. Daniel then, with one hand, took hold of me and used the other hand to swim us back toward the shore. As he was swimming, he said to me, "Start thanking the Lord now." With tears in my eyes, fear in my heart, and hope in my spirit, I repeatedly said, "Thank You, Jesus. Thank You, Jesus. Thank You, Jesus!"

Once we got out of the water, I said to him, "Why didn't you just leave me out there?" (as I had feared we both might end up dead). His response was "What would I look like going back home without you?" That was the day the thought was signed, sealed, and delivered: *this man really loves me!*

Now let's backtrack, and you take a wild guess on how my husband proposed to me. Take another one for how our wedding day went and another one for where we spent our honeymoon. Trust me—it was not a fairy-tale dream come true. To let him tell it, I must have been head over heels for him, as I willfully went along with concocting and following through with the ill-conceived plan. However, all of those events happened in a matter of a few weeks.

As for the proposal, let's just say there was a question mark written in the steam of my bathroom mirror with a ring on the ledge underneath. We still go back and forth to this day on whether or not he actually truly proposed. The wedding planning went something like "I dare you to get married this coming Monday." The wedding day was held at the local justice of peace. Those in attendance

Teach Me What Mama Didn't Know

were the officiator, my husband in his fly gear (army fatigues), and me in a Sunday-best white dress. We got two strangers to witness our union because we didn't know we needed witnesses. The honeymoon was about ten minutes outside our army base; we were both in the military at the time. But hey, though the sequences that led up to our union didn't go as society deems as normal, decades later, we are still together. And I am literally laughing out loud at this very moment. Why? Because every time one of our children does something against the norm, I have to sit and say to myself, "Remember when you and Daniel got married after knowing each other for only a few short months?"

So back to the question about how long should one wait before getting married. You sure you want my opinion on that? I'm laughing out loud again. I'm sure if you asked one hundred people that same question, you would get one hundred different answers. Why? Because every person will answer the question according to how they feel and what they have experienced. I have my opinion, based on my own experience.

Yes, Daniel and I are doing great, with the help of the Lord. But as stated earlier, our marriage has had its share of bumps and bruises. Would I marry him if I had to do it all over again? Knowing now what I have been taught from our heavenly Father, I most definitely would. Bumps, bruises, and all, there is no one better suited for me. He's my soul mate indeed.

My answer about when to get married comes from my experience. My experience would tell you it is

Marriage and Parenting

definitely important to put God first in everything. My experience would tell you to seek financial and marital wisdom and counseling early on. My experience would also tell you that, just as you are supposed to get yearly doctor checkups, you should plan to get yearly financial and marital checkups to stay prepared for the things that come with being married. My experience would tell you to take every situation to the Lord in prayer; I did and still do.

Now, to put my experience aside and to be practical, I would say the answer to this question has more to do with the relationship between the two people than with the amount of time that has been spent together in the relationship. Some of the questions that should be asked among couples considering marriage are as follows:

1. Do we share the same spiritual beliefs?
2. Do we have common goals and similar tastes?
3. Are there established ideas of what roles each would fill in the relationship?
4. Do we want children or not?
5. What are our financial goals? Are both partners going to work?

Of course, there are more questions that one should ask before getting married. I'd recommend the book *1,001 Questions to Ask before You Get Married* by Monica Mendez Leahy. Another book is one my husband and I have given many people, *The 5 Love Languages* by Gary Chapman.

Seek God's Counsel

People are always going to have opinions about how you should live your life. What you should be when you grow up. What type of car you should drive. How you should wear your hair. What colors look better on you. Whom you should date and not date. Whom you should marry. And yes, when's the most appropriate time for you to get married. I have witnessed on many occasions people losing out on great potential spouses because of being concerned about what someone else might think. They've listened to some of the following opinions from other people:

- You haven't known each other long enough.
- Your family members are close friends (like family).
- You're too young.
- You're not ready.
- They're not the one for you.

I hope I am making myself perfectly clear when I say this: when it comes to *your* life and especially who you should marry, when, and where, no one's opinion

Marriage and Parenting

matters but yours and God's. The Bible says in Matthew 6:33 (ESV), "But seek first the kingdom of God and his righteousness, and all these things will be added to you."

> **NO ONE'S OPINION MATTERS BUT YOURS AND GOD'S**
>
>
>
> #TMWMDK

Now if you are professing you love the Lord but are living a life contrary to His Word, then yes, wisdom from wise counsel is definitely needed. But if you truly love the Lord and are living your life with a desire to please Him, then only two opinions matter—yours and the Lord's. The key thing I want you to get from Matthew 6:33 is *seek God's counsel first*!

Let me show you how hypocritical people can be. If someone were to say to me, "Angela, I'm getting married to this person that I've known only for a short period of time," my brain would be thinking, *You're going to do what?* Then of course I'd have to remember the sequence of events that led to my marriage. But let's say I waited a few years before I got married. I would probably find myself trying to talk the person out of marrying someone they just met. Why? Because that's what we as human beings do. We act as if we know what's best for someone else. So, again, I say—seek God first! He knows what's best for you, and those things you wish to happen will either be His will or not His will. You are ultimately the one who must live with your choices, so pray and choose wisely.

Just because I married my husband right away doesn't mean we have more or fewer problems than any other married couple. In counseling with people, I have concluded we all go through the same ups and downs. What makes the difference is how and with whom you go through life. The how and who refer to obedience to God's Word and yielding to the correction of the Holy Spirit.

The scripture that helps me in just about all my life situations, especially my marriage, is 2 Chronicles 7:14 (ESV): "If my people who are called by my name humble themselves, and pray and seek my face and turn from their wicked ways, then I will hear from heaven and will forgive their sin and heal their land."

How does this scripture help me? I have learned that if I don't humble myself to the gumption of the Holy Spirit, then I might as well forget about praying. Why? Because praying to God is going to humble me and remind me of what the Holy Spirit has been suggesting I do. Once I have humbled myself, I can effectively pray and seek God's hand, His guidance, His favor. Often when I pray about a situation, God humbles me and reminds me of my own wrongdoings. So humbleness is not always easy, but if you love the Lord and want to live the awesome, abundant life He has planned for you, then it's definitely worth it. Romans 8:28 (ESV) says, "And we know that for those who love God all things work together for good, for those who are called according to his purpose."

Humbleness is worth it because God has already written out the perfect plan for you. If you want to get married, then pray, meditate, take some time, and heart-to-heart listen to God's advice for you about the situation.

Marriage and Parenting

If you believe wholeheartedly you've found the perfect person for you, only seek God's approval. If you want to get married right away or years later, again, God has the fitting plan for your life. Talk to Him. He will share with you the details. In all you do and desire to have, I highly suggest you seek the Author and Creator of your perfect destination: God the Father.

The Bible has established in so many verses how deeply the Lord loves you. He's concerned about even the smallest details you are concerned with. A question I have asked through this book is, Do you really love the Lord? If the answer is yes, please always remember that praying to God is one thing, but meditating and following His precise instructions is a whole different level that will lead you to the steps He has toward your abundant life. Trust me. I have tried Him for myself, and He has never failed me. I only fail when I do it my way instead of His. The bottom line for marriage is that if you want to know whether you should get married, here are four scriptures that were referenced in "Fleeing Temptation":

1. 1 Corinthians 6:18–19 (ESV) (deals with fornication)
2. 1 Corinthians 7:8–9 (ESV) (deals with to be single or not to be)
3. Genesis 2:24 (ESV) (deals with being married)
4. Malachi 2:16 (ESV) (deals with divorce)

If you get married and discover you and your spouse are having marital differences (it happens to the best of marriages), don't let divorce be your immediate plan. According to 1 Corinthians 13:4 (ESV), "Love is patient and kind; love does not envy or boast; it is not arrogant."

With that said, choose to handle your differences through the eyes of love. Don't be too proud to ask for forgiveness, and please don't become disagreeable and arrogant. Choose to be your spouse's best friend. Take the situation you both are dealing with to the Lord in prayer; pray together. If you totally surrender it to the Lord, He *will* fix it.

Special Note

If you value yourself, give yourself time to figure out what you really like before choosing a mate. Explore life outside of your familiar, everyday circle. Why? Because about 95 percent of your happiness for the remainder of your life will be based around the person you marry. Value and love yourself enough to choose your mate wisely. For those who are already married, understand that God did not create you to be anyone's doormat. If there are conflicts in your marriage, work together to resolve the issues. Also, just like you go to the doctor if you are sick, be willing to seek professional counseling; my husband and I did on several occasions because we desired unbiased human mediators.

Also, if you find yourself giving advice to someone about if they should get married or not, or when they should get married, or even whom they should marry,

Marriage and Parenting

please do yourself and them a huge favor: take the time to pray with them, asking God to reveal His divine purpose. You are not the creator of their universe. You do not know the plans God has for them. Please, please, please remind them to seek the advice of the one whose advice matters the most, their heavenly Father.

Pray without Ceasing

> Fathers, do not provoke your children,
> lest they become discouraged.
> —Colossians 3:21 (ESV)

With the pregnancy of each of my children, I read plenty of what-to-expect books pertaining to having a baby. At that time, I didn't have anyone close in my life who could share with me wisdom and knowledge on child birthing. So the books did a great job with getting my husband and me prepared.

There were plenty of books that prepared us for the birth, labor, and taking care of them as babies. However, I have not come across one book that told my husband and me how to deal with the situations we experienced while raising them. I mean, what book effectively prepares you when you get a call while you're two hours away, on a field trip, with another one of your children, and someone on the other end tells you they are flying your child to the hand trauma facility because a portion of their finger has been cut off. Or what book prepares you for your children to tell you a person of another race chased them down with a car, then on foot through the

Marriage and Parenting

woods. Or the struggles your children experience while trying to figure out their place in life. Or when your child heads off to join the military. Or when your child has their first heartbreak. There were definitely a lot of things I had to take to the Lord in prayer.

No one but me knows the difficulty I had to go through internally whenever I had to leave my children in the care of another—praying every day they weren't handled inappropriately in any way. The only book that helped me let go and let God was the Bible.

This parenting portion of the book is not long because, as I said before, nothing really 100 percent prepares you for raising children. But I do have the following suggestions:

1) Build a community of reliable adults who have proven to be trustworthy and who will help mentor your children to do the right thing. These adults can be from your church, people you are close friends with, team coaches, mentors from the local Boys and Girls clubs, leaders from your workplace, and even young people who have graduated school and have become successful in achieving their goals.
2) Pray without ceasing.
3) As one of my husband's cousins told me her grandmother advised her, "Learn to pick your battles." Things not done the way you think they should have been done do not always require a response from you, but everything should be taken to the Lord in prayer.

Teach Me What Mama Didn't Know

Marriage and parenting is not always easy, but if you humble yourself, seek God's face, and remember love is patient and kind, marriage and parenting will be a joyful, rewarding life experience.

> **REMEMBER LOVE IS PATIENT AND KIND**
>
>
>
> #TMWMDK

Three Verses to Look Up and Personalize

1) 1 Corinthians 13:4–6

2) 1 Thessalonians 5:17

3) Romans 12:5

Speak into the Atmosphere Prayer

"Heavenly Father, thank You for teaching me about marriage and parenting. Thank You for reminding me to seek You first in every decision for all my relationships. Thank You that even in matters of the heart, You are ready to lead and guide me in the direction I should go that will lead me and my loved ones to an abundant life. Thank You for helping us to together walk by faith and not by sight. In Jesus's name, I pray. Amen."

Money

Be a Great Steward

You lazy fool, look at an ant. Watch it closely; let it teach you a thing or two. Nobody has to tell it what to do. All summer it stores up food; at harvest it stockpiles provisions. So how long are you going to laze around doing nothing? How long before you get out of bed? A nap here, a nap there, a day off here, a day off there, sit back, take it easy—do you know what comes next? Just this: You can look forward to a dirt-poor life, poverty your permanent houseguest!
—Proverbs 6:6–11 (MSG)

In my writing, I let the Holy Spirit guide me to what Bible verse I should use. Typically, I use the parallel Bible to compare verses and decide which version brings home the point of the section I'm working on. The Message Bible for Proverbs 6:6–11 made me say, "Ouch." I could hear the Holy Spirit saying, "That's exactly the point—ouch." Especially when I read the last verse, I thought, *That's kind of harsh*, but it's the truth. People, places, and things owe you nothing. To take it a little further, once you get to a certain age, even your parents owe you nothing! Your parents are human beings, just like you are, and they are trying to budget and successfully make ends meet, just like you should be. Money does not grow on trees, so if you laze around and make no attempt to prepare for today and your tomorrows, it will seem as if poverty is your permanent houseguest. Poverty as a houseguest is like a dreaded disease that won't go away, making life long and miserable. Ouch!

Growing up, being considered poor never crossed my mind. Besides the short stint when I was homeless and lived out of an old blue pickup truck, I for the most part had a roof over my head, food in my belly, and clothing on my back. Looking back, I can see where some may have classified me as being poor. Most of the time, my clothing came from secondhand stores or yard sales, or were passed down. However, I didn't feel the pressure to have the latest sneakers or the latest outfit, so what clothing I had didn't really matter.

Once, my brother and I had our picture taken and placed on the local Detroit Focus Hope Community pamphlet, but even that didn't faze me. They gave us large blocks of thick cheese, which was great for grilled cheese sandwiches, delicious, thick peanut butter, and

Money

some tasty farina that would jump out of the pot and burn the crap out of you if you weren't careful while stirring it.

During my younger years, someone might have considered me to be a nomad because we moved from state to state just about every year. I can remember being in Michigan for kindergarten through first grade. For a portion of my second-grade year, I was in Pennsylvania, then back to Michigan through the third grade. Fourth grade, I lived in Tennessee. Fifth and sixth grades, back to Michigan. Seventh grade, I attended Southwest Elementary in Tennessee. In eighth grade, I went to Joy Junior High in Michigan. In ninth grade, I was in Tennessee, Fayette Ware High School (home of the Wildcats). In tenth grade, I was in Michigan, Mackenzie High (home of Stag Nation). For eleventh and twelfth grades, I was in Michigan, Southfield Senior High (home of the Blue Jays). The constant moving around didn't matter much to me. As I got older, I started to realize it wasn't the norm, but who gets to classify what's normal other than the person with the experience?

In traveling place to place, I was in the care of several people. In Tennessee, the one I spent most time with was my great-grandmother Hattie. She was indeed a strong woman—physically, mentally, spiritually, and emotionally. Among all her great-grands, I don't think she had any favorites, but she did have a favorite TV show. When wrestling came on, she was all the way live. She loved having her hair washed and plaited, and her scalp scratched and greased. She lived in a home my great-grandfather built for her, made of concrete blocks. During the hot days, for fun, we kids would climb onto the tin roof and slide down to the ground. We'd climb back up and do it again, though the heat from the roof would give an intense burning sensation to our legs. When the house would get cold in the winter, Grandma would go out, chop wood, bring it in, and light it on fire in a potbelly wood stove. Not only did her hands chop wood, she would also draw water from the well that was right in her front yard. She taught us how to lower the bucket, listen for the sound to know the bucket was full, and then pull the chain with one hand following the other, while slinging the chain to wrap it around the chain post. I can vividly recall the excitement of that experience.

My great-grandmother was always making something out of nothing. Her blackberry pies, her unconditional love, her laughter, her cures for all things that might ail us. Feeling poor was not an option when I was in her presence. She knew how to make you focus on better days. So though I may have in my younger years spent a lot of days urinating in a chamber pot, defecating in an outhouse, and washing clothes with a washboard, I'm grateful for those experiences, as they taught me how to stay strong physically, mentally, spiritually, and emotionally in an unpredictable economy.

My great-grandmother may not have been rich, but she definitely had everything she needed and wanted. In my opinion, neither rich nor wealthy, she lived a great, fulfilling life. Why? Because she was a great steward over what she had.

Personal Finance

Being rich is usually defined as having great sums of money. Wealth, on the other hand, is typically defined as having not only great sums of money but many assets, without the stress of ever having to go to a job to pay bills. Yes, most wealthy people have bills, but their combined resources of money and assets last them a lifetime. And if they remain great stewards over what they have, they will never have to worry about financial stress.

I know most people do not desire to be rich and famous. I also know no one desires to be broke, busted, and disgusted. To keep from being broke, busted, and disgusted, can I sit here and tell you college is the answer? No. Can I tell you going into the military is the answer? No. I can't even tell you that landing a career job right out of high school is the way to go. Why not? Because there are people with college degrees who can't find a job in their field of study, and the only thing they have to show for their degree is the debt they acquired while attending school. There are veterans who served their country for years and can't find a decent job in the civilian world. There are also people, some athletes, for example, who have landed a wonderful career right out of high school and are presently bankrupt. So no matter what you become and how you get there, you must be a good steward over your finances.

How can you be a good steward over your money? First, start saving at a young age. The earlier you start, the more money you will have as you mature toward your retirement years. Don't know where to start? Start by asking someone you know who seems to be wealthy. Search the internet for topics such as "how to save money worksheets." One worksheet I find realistic for young savers is "52 Week Savings Challenge for Kids" found on momdot.com. This is perfect for children who do not have a regular job but receive allowances and financial gifts for birthdays, grades, chores, and so on.

START SAVING AT A YOUNG AGE

#TMWMDK

Second, when you become old enough to receive a paycheck, evaluate your income (paycheck) against your expenses (bills). Create a budget plan and stick to it. Have present and future saving goals and stick to them. Proactively monitor your financial accounts by accurately keeping track of funds going in and out of them. I can list a whole bunch of other things to do, but I'll narrow it down to this: take a personal finance class and seek the advice of highly recommended financial advisers.

I often hear people ask, "Why doesn't the primary school system teach personal finances?" If you were taught how to properly take care of your finances every year—say, as they teach language arts, math, and so on—you wouldn't be trapped in the debt system. The system is designed to have you always working, always needing, always living paycheck to paycheck, and always dependent on the next handout. Why? As long as you are operating in the system, others who have mastered their personal finances can, off your labor and hard work, be richer, never working and never needing. Though the system is designed to keep the average person barely surviving paycheck to paycheck, you can do something about the situation. You can become a better, more responsible manager of what you have now, starting where you are now. Again, seek the advice of highly recommended financial advisers.

> THE SYSTEM IS DESIGNED TO KEEP THE AVERAGE PERSON BARELY SURVIVING
>
>
>
> #TMWMDK

You can escape the system. I've heard people say, "Knowledge is power." You need strong personal finance knowledge, a plan, and the will to follow through. It's never too late to start, so start now! And once again, seek the advice of highly recommended financial advisers.

Minimalism

I am constantly evaluating my material world to see what I can get rid of. In an effort to become a minimalist, I have asked myself on several occasions, if I had to leave in an emergency, what is it I absolutely must have. Truthfully, the answer is my God, my phone, my friends, and my family.

I need my God because of obvious reasons, and to personalize what David said in Psalm 37:25, God has never forsaken or left me, His seed, begging for bread. Yes, I sometimes wonder if He went on vacation. Wonder if I've gotten too old for Him to consider blessing me. Wonder if He forgot my address to send the blessings to. But He has proven to always be an on-time God, so I know He hasn't forsaken me, and never will He.

I need my phone because, well, that's my access to the Bible, 911, the internet, and my music, things that bring me aid and soothing comfort. All the other material possessions in my household are simply wants.

I absolutely need my friends and family (not my coworkers, not my associates), those who have shown loyalty to me. I have learned I need them because no matter how life may try to twist and bend me, I will not

Money

be broken as long as I have them in my life. Someone is going to always show up with a much-needed hug, much-needed smile, and much-needed helping hand.

Side note: remember to always create good relationships. Ecclesiastes 4:12 (ESV) says, "And though a man might prevail against one who is alone, two will withstand him—a threefold cord is not quickly broken."

Having nice things is great, but don't let it lead you to dreading life. It's a known fact that the average person is one to two delayed paychecks from having their car repossessed, credit score destroyed, or becoming homeless. Here are some tips to help determine if you are an average person or not. These are the tips I've learned to consider before purchasing anything.

Ask yourself the following:
1) Am I contributing regularly toward the building up of the kingdom of God through tithes and offerings?
2) Will my next purchase keep me from contributing tithes and offerings?
3) Are my bills caught up?
4) Do I have at least three to six months of finances saved for my bills in case of a financial emergency?
5) Are there adequate finances saved toward my individual and family goals?

If you can answer yes to all five questions above, then congratulations; you are well above average and are doing better than the majority of people in the world.

Teach Me What Mama Didn't Know

If you've answered at least one no and you do not desire to get caught in the system, perhaps it's time to try restarting by being a minimalist until you get where you desire to be financially. This means if you have to have only seven outfits and two pairs of shoes now, so that you can have whatever you want later without the financial stress, so be it.

Get your financial priorities in order. Start now and start where you are. I've seen plenty of people with sincere determination pull themselves out of a huge financial deficit. It doesn't take much effort. It does, however, take you being transformed by the renewing of your mind. Renew your mind by changing your spending and saving habits.

> START NOW AND START WHERE YOU ARE
>
> #TMWMDK

In seeking the Father's face, I have definitely been taught some things about money I wish I'd known when I first started out as a young adult. My first career was as a soldier in the United States Army. I had guaranteed twice-a-month payments on the first and the fifteenth for four years. The military provided me with room and board, so I didn't have to pay for my food or housing. They also provided me with clothing (uniforms), so I didn't have to worry about work clothing either. As I got older, I often wondered, *Just what did I do with my money during those four years?* I guess I was out there living like there was no tomorrow. Now I'm wishing someone would have taken me by the hand and shown me how to be financially responsible. It's what I do with my kids and anyone who will let me help them get their financial goals in order.

I started financial education early with my children. In their early teens, I ordered them prepaid bankcards. Our bank allowed me to create for them prepaid bank accounts through which my husband and I would give them money as needed. The reason we felt this was important was to start them off early knowing how to manage their finances using an ATM card. Basically, getting them to see that, no, you cannot just walk up to an ATM like it's a money tree and request all the money you desire; you must actually have money in your account. Showing them how to withdraw money from an ATM also helped us teach them about bank fees and other important things one needs to know about having a bank account.

As they've grown into adulthood, we've created for them seven bank accounts with the desire to help them balance their finances between paying their bills and personal spending. The accounts have each been given nicknames so they know what funds are for which activity. Their accounts are labeled Paycheck, Bills, Car Maintenance, Long-Term Savings, Stock, Personal Spending, and Secure Credit Card. Seven accounts may seem like a lot to someone, but here are the concepts we try to instill in them:

1) Paycheck: This is where your paycheck should be direct deposited. This account is set up to automatically transfer into the other six accounts.

2) Bills: Funds are transferred into this account to cover monthly bills—nothing more, nothing less. (Tithes and offerings are included in this account.)
3) Car Maintenance: This is for things like oil changes, car washes, new tires, brakes, and so on. A small portion of the paycheck is deposited monthly so that these normal, expected expenses won't appear so unexpected and throw the financial balance off.
4) Long-Term Savings: A percentage of the paycheck is deposited here to save toward major future payments. For example, a home or car down payments.
5) Stock: It's great to invest for the purpose of having another stream of income to aid toward financial freedom. Speaking of investing, if you are employed and your company offers savings plans such as 401(k), employee stock purchase plan, and so on, do your research and invest in those plans. They present other opportunities to get free money.
6) Secure Credit Card: Absolutely for emergencies only. True unexpected situations.
7) Personal Spending: This is the only place to go for available cash. All other cash is accounted for. Funds in this account can be spent freely.

The prior list is a laid-out suggestion for my children and those who have sought my help with getting their finances in order. Again, seven accounts can seem like a bit much. But they are in place to automate the income and outcome of the budget until they understand for themselves the importance of being a good steward over their finances.

It's Okay to Say No

As a Sunday school teacher, I've created my own curriculum, and one of the things I've incorporated in my class is teaching the students about money management. Every fourth Sunday, we play the Dave Ramsey "Act Your Wage" game. The game starts by having users randomly select three debt cards and one life card. The debt cards may have realistic debt, such as credit cards and bank and student loans. All debt must be paid off before a player can win the game. The life card may range from occupations such as a plumber to a scientist. The object of the game is to be the first person to get out of debt while moving around the game board. As you maneuver around each spot, you land on realistic, everyday life situations, such as making an extra payment on the electric bill because the kids left the lights on, as well as being laid off. Playing this game gives me a great opportunity to discuss being financially sound, refraining from debt, and building wealth.

Often when the students pull a "give" card, I remind them of the words my aunt Beverly once said to me: "How can you bless someone if you can't bless yourself?" I tell them to never let anyone make them

Money

feel guilty about not participating in their fundraisers. I inform them there is going to come a time in their lives when people are going to want them to buy from them—things such as cookies, gadgets, and wrapping paper, among other things. I let them know the quickest way to go broke is by not knowing how to say no. Yes, I know the Bible says in Luke 6:38 (ESV), "Give, and it will be given to you. Good measure, pressed down, shaken together, running over, will be put into your lap." That scripture does not pertain to giving to someone's cause. Nor does it pertain to buying people gifts. Those are two things we can always be guilt-tripped into participating in.

I go a little further and explain to them they want to ensure their current finances will be able to support them in their retirement years. Yes, it's okay to buy gifts and give to others' causes but only after doing a few checks and balances. The first check and balance is asking yourself the five questions listed earlier in this section. I tell them the second check and balance is, if you cannot take the same amount you are giving someone and put that exact amount in your long-term savings, you need to lower the amount of your contribution. For example, if I am considering giving Sally fifty dollars today and do not have fifty dollars to move over to my long-term savings account, then I need to reconsider how much I'm giving. The financial goal is not to become broke through gift giving. So perhaps, if I really want to give to Sally, then I can break that amount down to give her twenty-five dollars, and put twenty-five in my savings.

Always remember this: loyal friends and family should never make each other feel obligated or bad about giving and receiving. If you don't have it to give but really want to give something, consider giving the gift of your time, lending a helping hand. Everyone has some project they need an extra set of hands for; quality time is always a great gift.

> **LOYAL FRIENDS AND FAMILY SHOULD NEVER MAKE EACH OTHER FEEL OBLIGATED**
>
>
>
> #TMWMDK

Maintain Good Credit

The following is a list of financial information I wish I had known when I was starting as a young adult:

Credit Score (Do Not Let Anyone Mess Up Your Credit)

Credit scores are a point system that can range from 300 to 850. An 850 score is like getting an A on a test. On the other hand, a score of 300 would be seen as an F. Some things that can lower your credit score are not paying your bills on time, having too much credit, or having too little credit (you've got to find that healthy balance between too much and too little). Oddly but true, closing credit accounts can also lower your score. It's best to not use the credit you no longer need, rather than calling the creditor and asking them to cancel/close your account.

I did not know there was such a thing called a credit score until I went to purchase my first car. Up to that point, I had indulged in several credit cards and department store cards, cosigned for small loans for others, and so on. The good thing was I always paid my bills on time. So I was able to purchase my first car without a cosigner. Had I not kept up with my bills, I would be telling a different story.

Your credit score determines if lenders will grant you the funds to make major purchases, such as a home or car, take out business loans, and more. It also determines the interest rate at which you'll be paying the loan back. The lower your credit score, the higher the interest rate. High interest rates mean higher repayments; this can have you in a world of debt. Trying to pay that debt off can stress you out.

Also, some major corporations use credit scores to determine if you get hired as an employee. Therefore, sometimes a bad credit score can prevent you from landing your dream job.

Though I mentioned I once cosigned for small loans for others, I realized along my journey that doing that is *not* a smart idea. Things happen. People lose their income and therefore can't pay the loan back, and sometimes people just don't plan to pay it back. Tread wisely, be smart in your credit decisions, and do not let anyone mess up your credit. If you desire to be a good steward and live at least financially comfortable, then it is a must you maintain good credit.

Credit Cards (Secure Credit Card)

I wish someone had told me credit cards were not designed to be my financial friends. I wasn't credit card crazy, but I did have a few, along with a few department

Money

store cards. For me, it was the fact that I had them and paid them off, but I had no idea how interest rates for credit cards worked. I therefore paid way more than I should have for items I bought. Buying a bag of chips that normally costs around ninety-nine cents can easily, because of interest, end up costing five dollars to twenty or more. (Side note: never buy chips and everyday items on credit cards.) Now that my heavenly Father has taught me better through experience, I am a firm believer that credit cards should only be used for dire emergencies. My husband and I have also informed our kids to stay away from credit cards and invest in a secure credit card only. In my opinion, credit cards are for temporarily fixing a problem (want and or need) but can lead to a much more permanent and destructive financial problem.

Home Buying (Apartment)

I wish someone had strongly encouraged us not to buy a big house. We purchased our home with the thought of ensuring our kids had their own rooms. Well, our kids are all just about out of the nest, but the electric bill and house payments remain. We could have definitely accomplished our home-buying goal with a smaller home. Although God surely blessed us and we can pay for the home, a smaller one would mean much smaller monthly mortgage payments, lower utility bills, and more money in the savings for other pleasurable things.

During my childrearing years, I actually wished I lived in an apartment. Why?

- Less upkeep. Living on almost two acres of land is a beast to keep maintained.
- Not having to be responsible for the maintenance. It's always great when someone else must pay to have the plumbing, electric, and appliances fixed.
- Flexibility to move around and experience different environments. You can always get the house later, when you're ready to retire and settle in one particular area. Or don't buy one at all. It's not like you can take that $250,000+ home with you to the grave.

Please fully understand there are pros and cons to every major purchasing decision. The point I would like to drive home is *there are options*.

Car Buying (Lease, Trade In, Complete Purchase)

I wish someone had told me to save for a car. The more money you save to put toward a down payment, the less you must pay in the long run and the better interest rate you can negotiate for. As for buying a car, people have different opinions about if you should buy the car new or used. It costs a lot of money to fix something that's mechanically wrong with a car. New cars typically come with a warranty for three years or thirty-two thousand miles. Or you can get an extended

Money

warranty of seven years or one hundred thousand miles, whichever comes first (the years or the miles). If the car is still under warranty, then the warrantor pays for most major repairs. If the car is used, most likely there is no warranty. So if something breaks that costs $1,000, then if there is no warranty, you will have to pay for those repairs.

There are so many options when it comes to car buying. Leasing a car, you never really own the car, but you get the chance to drive a different car every one to two years. When buying a car, you can buy it with the thought of paying for it over time, or trading it in later for something else without paying the first car completely off. Or you can pay the car completely off and hold on to it for many years. The point is there are options. My husband and I have purchased cars, paid them off, and passed them down to our children to use. For my next car. I desire to lease it. The choice is yours, but the choice should be made according to what will lead you to financial freedom, not what will cause you to remain in long-term financial bondage. Again, the point is there are options.

Investing (If You Do It Right, You Can Borrow Money from Yourself)

With the help of the Father, I figured out the importance of investing. I am not going to sit here and tell you I know all there is to know about investing. But I will tell you it's important to make your money work for you. Investing is like taking one seed of corn, planting it in the field, watering it, and watching it multiply to several stalks of corn. It's like getting free money. Who does not like free, and who does not like money? I can't give you investment strategies for becoming the next millionaire. But I can tell you that you can become a multimillionaire sooner than later by letting your money work for you. I can also tell you two gurus I've found easy to understand on the subject of investment are Phil Town and Daniel R. Solin. Dave Ramsey is someone I have found it easy to understand when talking about getting out of debt and personal financial management.

Gift Giving (You Will Never Be Able to Buy Someone's Love, Affection, and Appreciation)

The quickest way to go broke is to feel obligated to buy everyone in your circle a gift. In my opinion, among my friends, I am the worst gift giver. It comes from the heart, but it might be wrapped in a plastic shopping bag. Or they may receive a handwritten note to go with the gift versus a card. Why? Because my thought is, if I must buy wrapping paper and a card, it's going to be taken away from the cost of the gift. So where they may have initially gotten something they really wanted, they may now just get a pack of pencils. Yes, I'm that type of gift giver, but it comes from the heart, and those who love me understand and accept that about me. Besides, in my opinion, the best way to show someone appreciation is to spend time with them.

Advice corner for young kids: If the gift is for a kid, don't spend more than ten dollars. If you can't think of anything creative, then give them the ten dollars along with a handwritten note. And if they don't appreciate the gift, they aren't really your friends. Also, parents will not always have it to give for each and every one of your friends. If you absolutely, positively feel that you must buy a friend a gift, then think of creative ways you can earn the money to do so.

Two Final Points

1) You have options. There are pros and cons to every scenario. The bottom line is you must make the right option for your financial situations and goals. My point in listing the things I wish I had known is just that. I did not know there were other options in each scenario. Another doable option is to save your money and buy the things you want—with cash, not credit. Yes, it's doable! Everything is possible if you have a plan and stick to it.

2) Money is not the root of all evil. I can guarantee you that you are going to hear people say, "Money is the root of all evil." That saying is a total misquote of 1 Timothy 6:10 (ESV): "For the love of money is a root of all kinds of evils. It is through this craving that some have wandered away from the faith and pierced themselves with many pangs." The scripture is plainly letting us know it is the *love* of money that is the root of all evil, not money itself. Get your money, but don't let money get you! Don't let it get you turning your back on God. Don't let it get you pulling down the next person, wanting to claim status for yourself. Don't let it get you thrown in jail or homeless. Don't let it get you trying to claim a temporary status to impress people, those who couldn't care less about the stress that going into debt will cause you.

There is absolutely nothing wrong with becoming rich or wealthy. Get your money. But make sure you keep your personal finances in order. Being a good steward over what you have is one of the things that will help you live a less stressful life.

KEEP YOUR PERSONAL FINANCES IN ORDER

#TMWMDK

Three Verses to Look Up and Personalize

1) Hebrews 13:5

2) Ecclesiastes 5:10

3) Malachi 3:10

Speak into the Atmosphere Prayer

"Heavenly Father, thank You for teaching me to be a better steward over the things You have blessed me with. Thank You for teaching me to be proactive and wise over all my financial decisions. Thank You for helping me set financial goals and helping me stick to a budget. Thank You for always reminding me to never worry about tomorrow. In Jesus's name. Amen."

…
Religion versus Relationship

Exodus 20:3 (ESV)

Traditions

You shall have no other gods before me.
—Exodus 20:3 (ESV)

My mother, Barbara, once informed me that one of the best things that ever happened to her was when a cousin whom she is very close with invited her to church. According to my mom, this was the start toward her brighter days. Quite naturally, with my mother going to church, I went with her as well. I had always gone to church with someone, said my grace, and prayed at night. However, it wasn't until I started going to these services with her that I discovered something different. Like there was a pull on my whole being toward something greater. Churches I attended before this one had so many

Teach Me What Mama Didn't Know

traditional nonbiblical rules. Those rules caused me to be tense and afraid of not getting things right, like when to stand, when and where to sit. I was unsure of how to engage in church activities, like when to clap and when to rejoice. The services with my mother were liberating. You were free to sing, free to express your love toward God, free to praise, free to worship, free to read the Bible and pray to the Lord for yourself.

Again, I always went to church. I fellowshipped with various denominations (though at the time I didn't know there was such a thing as denominations). I used to categorize churches as, this is where the young people go, this is where the old people go, this is where African Americans go, this is where Asians go, this is where Caucasians go, and so on and so forth.

Speaking of where the old people go, I remember once going to a church where there were about five people—well, perhaps seven, including my mother and myself. Outside of my mother and I, everyone had to have been well into their seventies, if not eighties. The church was extremely small and located off a dirt road in Tennessee. That church service was the most uncomfortable church experience I ever had. I cannot begin to tell you what was preached, what was sung, or what else was done during the service. Though they seemed to be having a great time, I was scared to death. Again, I can't say for sure why; perhaps it was because I was in an environment I was not used to. They were singing hymns, I guess. Being from Detroit, I was used to hearing people in church singing the latest songs being

Religion versus Relationship

played on the radio. So imagine seventy- to eighty-year-olds singing songs, not from a book but from memory, and me having no clue what they were saying. You have to understand: in Tennessee, I learned a lot about superstitions, along with various ghost tales. So, at some point, I started wondering whether they were casting spells over me. I'm so glad my mother never took us back there.

Another church memory happened in Detroit. This time, it was not only me and my mother; my oldest brother was there as well. At the altar was someone the preacher declared as possessed. I must admit the person was definitely acting like it. The preacher asked everyone in the congregation to start praying. I recall seeing my mother standing, praying with her hands stretched forth. My brother was a cool teenager; he was not feeling the whole church thing, so he was not praying at that moment. I did not want whatever was in that person to jump into my brother or me. So I stood as close as possible to him and started, under my breath, calling on the name Jesus. I said "Jesus" so fast and about a hundred times; someone might have thought I was speaking in tongues. I was young in my faith at the time; I had not made it to the part of the Bible where it talked about Jesus casting out demons and instructing His disciples to do the same. I am not sure if we were going to any form of Bible study at the time, so that was definitely another moment when I had no clue what was going on and was afraid.

Teach Me What Mama Didn't Know

Those were two rare occasions in my life. I definitely have not been able to erase them from my memory. Nonetheless, most of the time I went to church with my mom, I got to experience the love and joy of Jesus through praise and worship, along with various prayer services. It was definitely what I needed before I even knew I needed it. I too can say, like my mother did, getting to know Jesus for myself was the starting point toward my brighter days. The more we went to worship services, the more I felt His presence in my life and the more I wanted to know about Him, so I began to study the Bible for myself. I studied the Bible like I was studying the most amazing bibliography, trying to discover all the amazing attributes of my heavenly Father. I studied like I was studying a will left for an inheritor, trying to figure out the treasures He had for me in His will. I studied using study Bibles, biblical commentaries, and concordances. The more I studied, the more I became in wonder and awe of the Lord—*Wow, He loves me and calls me friend*.

As I got older, I realized churches are not necessarily categorized by race but mostly by denomination. I also realized Christians affiliate themselves with different denominations for various reasons that matter to them. As a Christian, I'm often asked my opinion about different denominations. My response has always been from my perspective, which is that church denominations are like personalities. Some people like quiet and reserved environments. Some like to be in places where there is always a church service going on. Some do not like to

Religion versus Relationship

make decisions, so they would much rather you tell them when, what, and how to do something. I like feeling free to worship, so I prefer nondenominational churches. My personal preference is just that, *my* preference. Why is it my preference? To me, it's less about traditions and more about being free to praise and worship the Lord in the beauty of His holiness. It's like getting to know and experience your favorite things for yourself. I am always studying the Word of God for myself. I am constantly drawing nigh to Him, constantly thanking Him for desiring to have a relationship with me. I love Jesus, and I love worshipping the Lord as He desires. In John 4:23 (ESV), it says, "But the hour is coming, and is now here, when the true worshipers will worship the Father in spirit and truth, for the Father is seeking such people to worship him."

As mentioned earlier, I have created my own Sunday school curriculum. I often advise the students not to follow human-ordained religious traditions. I inform them there will come a time on their Christian journey when some people will try to make them more concerned with the traditions of the church than their relationship and discipleship with Christ. I prepare them to be brave enough to ask those people to show them where the Bible says they should or shouldn't do this or that when it comes to serving the Lord. I tell them not to accept and follow through with others' misquoted references to God's Word, as some people misquote for selfish gains, and others may misquote due to hearsay. Here are a few examples of misquoted scriptures:

Teach Me What Mama Didn't Know

1. Spare the rod; spoil the child.
   a. This is a misquote of Proverbs 13:24 (ESV): "Whoever spares the rod hates his son, but he who loves him is diligent to discipline him."
2. You take one step; God takes two.
   a. This is a misquote of James 4:8 (ESV): "Draw near to God, and he will draw near to you. Cleanse your hands, you sinners, and purify your hearts, you double-minded."
3. Prayer changes things.
   a. This is a misquote of James 5:16 (ESV): "Therefore, confess your sins to one another and pray for one another, that you may be healed. The prayer of a righteous person has great power as it is working."
   b. To elaborate on this, God does answer prayers, but I do not want you to think you are being punished just because you prayed about something and God didn't make it happen as you saw fit or as soon as you desired. He answers prayer according to His will. Part of His will is the plans He has for your life (Jeremiah 29:11).
4. The race is not given to the swift nor to the strong but to the one that endures to the end.
   a. This is a misquote of Ecclesiastes 9:11 (ESV): "Again I saw that under the sun the race is not to the swift, nor the battle to the strong, nor bread to the wise, nor riches to the intelligent,

Religion versus Relationship

nor favor to those with knowledge, but time and chance happen to them all."
   b. I used to misquote this one all the time, as it was heresy passed down to me. Then one day I was studying God's Word and realized I was misquoting the Bible.
5. Study to show yourself approved.
   a. This is a misquote of 2 Timothy 2:15 (KJV): "Study to shew thyself approved unto God, a workman that needeth not to be ashamed, rightly dividing the word of truth."
   b. This scripture does start as stated, but some people misquote it by saying that if you want to be approved by God, you have to study.

I find it important for everyone to know the difference between religion worship (tradition) and relationship/discipleship worship. Too much tradition can have you missing out on the most important message of the Bible, being born again and the totality of the love of God.

Tradition can also have you stressed out when it comes to the idea of serving the Lord. For me, when the tradition of just going to church changed to the desire of getting to know more about Jesus for myself, I cannot totally express the awesomeness I feel when I think about the supernatural change that happened in my life. When I sought after my heavenly Father with my whole heart, He restored me and began revealing the plan He always had for my life.

Teach Me What Mama Didn't Know

There are a lot of churches where people put more focus on traditions than they do on true discipleship. For example, the focus is on what day you should have worship services, what you can and cannot wear, where you can and cannot sit, whether or not women and children are allowed to serve in the church. Don't get me wrong. The Bible does speak on some of those things I just mentioned. However, when the environment of the worship service is more about those things than it is about God's grace and mercy, it can cause stress and quickly cause one to lose their faith, ultimately losing out on life abundantly.

God Loves You

If you desire to live an abundant life, a life full of love, joy, and peace, I strongly advise you to study the Bible for yourself. If you're not sure where to start with your biblical studies, I suggest starting with the New Testament, mixing in some readings from Proverbs and Psalms. From there, I suggest moving forward with the Old Testament. There are plenty of good books available for guiding you in how to study the Bible. Tim LaHaye's book *How to Study the Bible for Yourself* ranks among one of my favorites. Also, when you are not sure about something you have heard or read, you can search the internet with starter phrases such as "What does the Bible say about …"

Trust me when I say your life will never be the same when you seek God with your whole heart, getting to know the Father, Son, and the Holy Spirit on a personal level. I cannot find the right descriptive words to express the great joy and peace that will come into your life. Every time I think of the goodness of Jesus and all He has done for me, I go into a place of complete wonderment.

Whatever you do, do not let human-ordained traditions become your god. Again, read and study the

Teach Me What Mama Didn't Know

Bible for yourself. Life can sometimes be a hard, lonely place, so get to know Jehovah-Shalom, the one and only Lord of Peace. I highly encourage you to get to know the treasures laid out for you in the will of God. God desires a relationship with us more than religious traditional practices. He lets us know this in at least two scriptures. Hosea 6:6 (ESV) says, "For I desire steadfast love and not sacrifice, the knowledge of God rather than burnt offerings." Matthew 12:7 (ESV) says, "And if you had known what this means, 'I desire mercy, and not sacrifice,' you would not have condemned the guiltless."

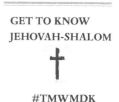

GET TO KNOW JEHOVAH-SHALOM

#TMWMDK

Above everything in this world, understand God loves you and desires a relationship with you more than religious practices.

How much He loves you can be seen in John 3:16 (ESV)" "For God so loved the world, that he gave his only Son, that whoever believes in him should not perish but have eternal life."

The Creator of the universe loves you so much. Romans 8:38–39 (ESV) says, "For I am sure that neither death nor life, nor angels nor rulers, nor things present nor things to come, nor powers, nor height nor depth, nor anything else in all creation, will be able to separate us from the love of God in Christ Jesus our Lord."

He desires you to love others as well. In 1 John 4:7–8 (ESV), it says, "Beloved, let us love one another, for love is from God, and whoever loves has been born of God

Religion versus Relationship

and knows God. Anyone who does not love does not know God, because God is love."

The heavenly Father is my go-to. I greatly desire a right relationship with the Father, so I often ask the Holy Spirit to search me and chastise me heavily on anything I might be doing to displease God. Why? Not only do I love the Lord, I am in love with Him. Though everything in my life hasn't been perfect, just as I am not perfect, He has never failed me. He keeps showing up when I need Him the most, always right on time, putting the pieces back together. So, yes, I turn to Him for everything. I depend on Him to be who He says He is, Jehovah-Mephalti (my Deliverer).

On this earth, you only live once. The best relationship you can have is one with your heavenly Father. If you work to get that relationship right, everything else will fall into place. If you are not sure how to study God's Word, join a Bible study group. Not sure with whom or where? Ask around. Someone can point you in the right direction. Always remember God desires a loving relationship with you more than traditional religious rituals.

Three Verses to Look Up and Personalize

1) Matthew 22:37

2) Luke 4:18

Teach Me What Mama Didn't Know

3) Hebrews 13:8–9

Speak into the Atmosphere Prayer

"Heavenly Father, thank You for teaching me to desire a relationship with You more than traditional worship. I know I am not perfect, but with the help of the Holy Spirit, I will refuse to purposely do anything not pleasing in Your sight. Thank You for always being my protector, provider, deliverer, and friend. Thank You for letting Your good and perfect will be done in my life. In Jesus's name. Amen."

Rewrite the Script

Romans 12:2 (ESV) & 2 Corinthians 5:17 (ESV)

Getting Directions

Do not be conformed to this world, but be
transformed by the renewal of your mind, that
by testing you may discern what is the will of
God, what is good and acceptable and perfect.
—Romans 12:2 (ESV)

Therefore, if anyone is in Christ, he is a new creation.
The old has passed away; behold, the new has come.
—2 Corinthians 5:17 (ESV)

I recall one day driving down the street, and the Lord began illustrating to me how the Bible is like the Christian's GPS system. As a minister, I was getting excited about this conversation because I felt the Lord was preparing me in advance for the next message I was to preach. Then came the next Sunday after the conversation with the Lord, and I heard my husband from the pulpit lightly touch on the subject of the GPS. So I said to the Lord, "There is no way I'm going to be able to go after the pastor with a message about the GPS system; people might think I'm copying His message."

Of course, I realized I wouldn't have to preach for some time. I was therefore hoping that by the time I did, no one would remember he mentioned it. Then a few Sundays after, another minister in our church got deep into the topic of God's Word being like a GPS system. So, by then, I thought, *Okay, Lord. Well, she pretty much covered what needed to be said*. Lo and behold, a bishop we fellowship with came to our church to preach. That day, I was responsible for copying the sermon onto a CD. I was given the paper on which the bishop wrote the sermon title, and the topic was "God's GPS." At that moment, I felt like I was living out the conversation between Eli and Samuel in 1 Samuel 3:3–10 (ESV):

> The lamp of God had not yet gone out, and Samuel was lying down in the temple of the LORD, where the ark of God was. Then the LORD called Samuel, and he said, "Here I am!" and ran to Eli and said, "Here I am, for you called me." But he said, "I did not call; lie down again." So he went and lay down. And the LORD called again, "Samuel!" and Samuel arose and went to Eli and said, "Here I am, for

Rewrite the Script

you called me." But he said, "I did not call, my son; lie down again." Now Samuel did not yet know the LORD, and the word of the LORD had not yet been revealed to him. And the LORD called Samuel again the third time. And he arose and went to Eli and said, "Here I am, for you called me." Then Eli perceived that the LORD was calling the boy. Therefore Eli said to Samuel, "Go, lie down, and if he calls you, you shall say, 'Speak, LORD, for your servant hears.'" So Samuel went and lay down in his place. And the LORD came and stood, calling as at other times, "Samuel! Samuel!" And Samuel said, "Speak, for your servant hears."

As I was typing "God's GPS" onto the label, I realized there was more to the initial conversation between God and me about the GPS. I immediately said to the Lord, "I feel You are trying to get my attention, so speak, Lord. Your servant hears." I went inside the sanctuary, sat on the back pew, and with pen and paper started taking serious notes, like it was about to be revealed to me where X marks the spot to my God-given treasures. As the bishop was preaching, this is what I heard from the Lord:

1) I am about to come in and shake things up.
2) Isaiah 30:21: "And your ears shall hear a word behind you, saying, 'This is the way, walk in it …'"

3) I am about to help you get back on track.
4) I have places for you to go and people to see. I want to take you somewhere.
5) I love you so much. I want you to experience the future I have planned for you.
6) No weapon formed against you shall prosper, and every tongue that rises up against you shall be condemned.
7) Get you a song you can sing to command your day so you remember you are blessed.
8) My promises for your life are yes and amen.
9) Reroute to the place I have for you.
10) When it looks like it's going the wrong way, be still and know that I am God.
11) You will eat the good of the land because you have been willing and obedient.
12) I am ready to bless your going out and coming in, bless everything you put your hands to.
13) You are on My radar. Know that I know you.
14) Remember that without faith it is impossible to please Me. Come what may, keep the faith!
15) I am a rewarder to those who diligently seek Me. Seek My face first in everything!
16) I will show Myself strong on your behalf.
17) I will be there when you need Me.
18) Everything is at My disposal when it comes to accomplishing My sovereign will and plan for your life (which means if I want to use a rooster to talk to you, then cock-a-doodle-doo).
19) I will do what I said in My Word.

Rewrite the Script

20) Continue to treasure My Word to the point you will purposely obey it.
21) Position yourself to be blessed. It is going to happen because you are in your place and you are loved by Me.
22) Jeremiah 29:11, "For I know the plans I have for you, declares the LORD, plans for welfare and not for evil, to give you a future and a hope."

I was sitting on that back pew like a kid at Christmas, with my mouth and eyes wide open, seeing so many treasures under the tree, thinking, *Oh my God! God is about to show up and show out in my life.*

- But I did not know I was going to be in a car accident before the wheels for my life's plan got to rolling (1).
- I did not know I was going to be out of work for two months with no pay (14).
- I did not know the blessings from friends and family and unexpected checks were going to pour in my life (11).
  I can list a scenario for every item during that two months when I was out of work and my body was in pain.
- I kept hearing the Holy Spirit remind me of what God already said (3).
- Whenever doubt tried to creep in (7).
- From the previous numbered list, I was constantly hearing the Lord say to me the following:

- When it looks like it's going the wrong way, be still and know that I am God.
- I am ready to bless your going out and coming in, bless everything you put your hands to.
- I will show Myself strong on your behalf.
- I will do what I said in My Word.
- For I know the plans I have for you, declares the LORD, plans for welfare and not for evil, to give you a future and a hope.

It was clearly time for me to get out the way and allow the Lord to do some new things.

I must admit, while I was in excitement for what I felt the Lord was about to do, I still in my mind was telling the Lord, *All these things sound great, but I still have a lot on my plate. Lord, I know what You are calling me to do, but I have so many responsibilities. I can't just drop what I'm doing now.* That's when the message of the GPS turned into "Rewrite the Script." It was like the Lord was giving me permission to drop everything and start my life all over again. I could hear God tell me He was about to do a new thing. "Behold, I am doing a new thing; now it springs forth, do you not perceive it? I will make a way in the wilderness and rivers in the desert" (Isaiah 43:19 ESV).

Imagine that! God putting a road in the wilderness and rivers in the desert! The one who made this world out of nothing can do anything at any time, as He has everything at His disposal! My God is an awesome God!

ROAD IN THE WILDERNESS AND RIVERS IN THE DESERT!

#TMWMDK

Rewrite the Script

Before we venture any further, let me explain to you the revelation I received when I asked the Lord what was meant by *rewrite the script*. This is what I heard: "You only live once here on this version of earth. And though there will be trials and tribulations from time to time, My ultimate desire is that you have an abundant life. If you are not experiencing life abundantly, to the fullest, then it's time to rewrite the script. Rewrite the screenplay you have put into production for your life." And so I moved from a place of GPS rerouting to "it's time to rewrite the script."

> For everything there is a season, and a time for every matter under heaven: a time to be born, and a time to die; a time to plant, and a time to pluck up what is planted; a time to kill, and a time to heal; a time to break down, and a time to build up; a time to weep, and a time to laugh; a time to mourn, and a time to dance; a time to cast away stones, and a time to gather stones together; a time to embrace, and a time to refrain from embracing; a time to seek, and a time to lose; a time to keep, and a time to cast away; a time to tear, and a time to sew; a time to keep silence, and a time to speak; a time to love, and a time to hate; a time for war, and a time for peace. (Ecclesiastes 3:1–8 ESV)

Teach Me What Mama Didn't Know

It was now time for me to rid myself of every person, place, and thing that continued to rob me of love, peace, and joy—everything that had me busy just for the sake of being busy.

Never Too Late

Now for those twenty-five years and younger, this book was written to help prepare you for adulthood. You, however, have got to purpose in your mind that you will succeed and accomplish everything you set out to do. Fully understand that people only have as much control over you as you allow them to have. Fully understand some people are just not going to like you, because they don't like themselves and their life circumstances. Fully understand some people in the Bible didn't like Jesus, but He didn't allow them to stop Him from doing what He wanted to do. Don't let the negativity from people, places, and things stop you. If you have moments in your life when you are beginning to doubt yourself, because you feel you weren't better prepared, remember that God says … item 6 ("No weapon formed against you shall prosper, and every tongue that rises up against you shall be condemned") and item 10 ("When it looks like it's going the wrong way, be still and know that I Am God") and item 15 ("I am a rewarder to those who diligently seek Me. Seek My face first in everything"). Always, always, always have a talk with Jesus. Be still and listen to and follow His guidance for you. Study God's Word, and obey His commands.

Teach Me What Mama Didn't Know

Now, to everyone, maybe you feel like you are already too far along on this journey, and you realize you are living other people's plans and goals for your life. Perhaps material possessions are trying to anchor you down and keep you from your life-changing goals. Maybe because of temptations you indulged in, you don't feel worthy and have robbed yourself of self-love. You may have also fallen into the trap of being all you can be for the dreams and hopes of others. You may feel like you flunked in marriage, parenting, and money. Maybe up to this point, your practice of religious traditions has been greater than your love for God. The good news is God loves you so much; every second of the day, you can rewrite your script and start over. So start over!

> EVERY SECOND OF THE DAY, YOU CAN REWRITE YOUR SCRIPT
>
>
>
> #TMWMDK

I cannot begin to tell you how many times I've gone to the altar and rededicated my life to the Lord. However, it doesn't matter to God; what matters is that we recognize we've been given the privilege to start over.

David in Psalm 37:25 (ESV) says, "I have been young, and now am old, yet I have not seen the righteous forsaken or his children begging for bread." Notice the essential words in the Amplified version, "those in right standing with God." As long as you are in right standing with God, He will never leave you or forsake you. And realize that Jesus says in John 10:10 (ESV), "The thief comes only to steal and kill and destroy. I came that they may have life and have it abundantly."

Rewrite the Script

The question is, What is keeping you from rewriting your script and starting all over?

I can share with you what kept me from rewriting my script: fear. And yes, I know it says in Isaiah 41:10 (ESV), "Fear not, for I am with you; be not dismayed, for I am your God; I will strengthen you, I will help you, I will uphold you with my righteous right hand."

But guess what? That didn't keep me from fearing. I was declaring that I was standing on the promises of God while still fearing. See, what God showed me He was about to do in my life had me saying, "But, Lord, I need my job to help with the bills. What if my husband gets frustrated with me not working forty hours per week? How will this affect my daughter's chances of going to the college she wants to go to? What if my grandkids suffer because of this leap of faith?" I was all the way in the future and didn't even have grandchildren at the time. I was completely going against the Word of God and began worrying about tomorrow. But I realized my God had never left me or forsaken me, so I said boldly, "Let's do this!"

Whatever is trying to hold you back, declare at this moment, "Enough is enough!" It's never too late to start over again. March forth. Fast. Pray. Rewrite the script. Start your life over again.

Three Verses to Look Up and Personalize

1) Romans 10:9

2) Romans 12:2

3) 2 Corinthians 5:7

Speak into the Atmosphere Prayer

"Heavenly Father, thank You for loving me. Thank You, Holy Spirit, for reminding me to renew my mind. Thank You for transformation. Thank You for a fresh start. In Jesus's name, I pray. Amen!"

By the Grace of God, She Made It

There once lived a timid little girl. She had in her lifetime been abused, neglected, and rejected by many. She was fed and believed the lies that she would never be worth anything to anyone. So she used to consider putting an end to her very existence. That was until one day she heard about a man named Jesus. This Jesus the Christ loved her more than she could ever imagine. She took the steps to invite Him into her heart and asked Him to be Lord over her life. From that very moment, she began to see the dawning of new days filled with love, peace, and joy. She began to study His Word and began demanding back everything the enemy tried to steal from her. I was once that little girl; my name is no longer retard, it is no longer useless, and it is no longer cursed!

Rewrite the Script

My name is Angela Baker-Ward, and I am daughter to the King. I will, through prayer and by firmly standing on God's Word, rise above every negative thing and keep my love, joy, and peace. I am a victorious overcomer, and the Lord my Father, my God, has taught me what Mama didn't know. Like Isaiah 50:4 (ESV) says, "The Lord GOD has given me the tongue of those who are taught, that I may know how to sustain with a word him who is weary. Morning by morning he awakens; he awakens my ear to hear as those who are taught."

My Father has taught me, and it is my pleasure and duty to teach and speak life into everyone I meet. You, my friend, shall live and not die! You are more than a conqueror! Stand firmly on the Word of God!

Go—bring to reality your hopes, dreams, visions, and goals! Walk by faith and not by sight! You got this!

The "Self-Love" chapter was amazing. I loved it and believe many people need to read it.
—Kimberly (teenager)

Reading "Friends, Family, and Them" was very deep. It hit on so many things I have been dealing with. I believe this has opened my eyes and given me a new outlook on things. From start to finish, I was locked in. This was very helpful, and I would recommend others read it.
—Admed (college student)

Teach Me What Mama Didn't Know is biblically based, heartfelt advice, some drawn from explicit exploration of painful life experiences spiritually interpreted to transform trauma to triumph.
—Dr. Donna, M.D.

To contact the author for speaking engagements visit: www.wardministries.com

To journey along with Angela during this amazing love, peace and joy experience visit: www.angelabakerward.com or follow #TMWMDK on social media outlets.

Notes